# Billy Baldwin

## *The Great American Decorator*

Adam Lewis

*Foreword by* **Albert Hadley**

**RIZZOLI**
NEW YORK

New York · Paris · London · Milan

For these six,

five who knew Billy Baldwin,

Deeda and Bill Blair,

Edward Lee Cave,

Albert Hadley, and

Harry Hinson,

and one who worked
to make the book a reality,

Thom Chu

5

*The New York City apartment of Woodson Taulbee. The Henri Matisse drawing over the sofa was a gift to Taulbee from Baldwin. Together Baldwin and Taulbee developed the design of the cotton fabric, "Foliage," that is used on the sofa and Baldwin slipper chair. Photo by Horst.*

# Contents

# I Remember Billy

Adam Lewis's book documenting the life of Billy Baldwin with authority, candor, charm, and even humor prompted me to remember my admiration for Billy Baldwin and our long friendship.

Before World War II, during my school years in Nashville, Tennessee, I worked for A. Herbert Rogers, one of the most respected interior decorators in the South. Under his guidance I received important and meaningful training. At this early age I already knew that I was destined for a career in design and my goal was to live in New York City. Each month I devoured the latest issue of *House & Garden, Interiors,* and *Vogue* when they arrived in the mail. I dreamed of being a part of the interior decorating community whose work was featured in these magazines. When I was drafted for military service in 1942, my pursuit of interior decorating was put on hold until the war was over.

In the late summer of 1947, I finally made my first visit to New York. My agenda was to explore the city and meet face-to-face the interior decorators who had long been my inspiration, my idols. I wasn't looking for a job. I knew I wasn't ready for that. I just wanted to meet these professionals who had lit the way and discuss a career in interior decorating.

William Pahlmann, known as the "Merlin of Decoration," was the director of the interior decoration department at Lord & Taylor. He was one of the people with whom I wanted to have an interview. I also wanted to meet James Amster, George Stacey, Rose Cumming, and Eleanor Brown, the founder and director of McMillen, Inc. Paramount on my list were Ruby Ross Wood and her associate, Billy Baldwin.

When I called Mrs. Wood's office, the secretary told me that Mrs. Wood had not returned from her summer in the country but Mr. Baldwin would be happy to see me. When I arrived at the office, which was on an upper floor of a building on East Fifty-seventh Street, I was greeted by a stylish sign on the door, Ruby Ross Wood, in the form of a freehand drawing by Cecil Beaton. Beaton was one of my favorite players in the world of art and design.

I shall never forget Billy coming into the very glamorous showroom where he extended a cordial welcome and invited me into his office. There was no air-conditioning in those days, just electric fans, and it was a very hot day. Billy was not wearing a coat, but he had on a beautiful tie and looked spiffy and very handsome. As our conversation progressed, he expressed a sincere interest in me and my desire to be a part of the New York interior decorating community. He suggested that I stay in touch with him when I returned to the city. As luck would have it, several days later I was walking on East Fifty-seventh Street and I saw Billy with Mrs. Wood. From quite some distance he hailed me to join them. Introducing me to Mrs. Wood, he said, "Mr. Hadley is the young man I told you about."

Getting to meet the venerable Mrs. Archibald Brown was not easy. George Stacey, a close friend of hers, arranged for me to have an appointment. Mrs. Brown's firm, McMillen, Inc., was one of the most prestigious decorating firms in America. When I arrived, she was charming but very businesslike and told me immediately that she did not hire any

decorator who was not a graduate of Parsons School of Design. Mrs. Brown was a Parsons graduate, a member of the school's board of directors, and a close personal friend of the school's president, Van Day Truex. Naturally I was prompted to visit Parsons, then at 136 East Fifty-seventh Street. The school was impressive. I knew immediately that Parsons was the school for me.

My Parsons education began the following summer, in 1948, when I attended the twelve-week summer program in France and Italy. When I returned to New York that fall to begin classes, I discovered that Billy was a visiting lecturer and critic at Parsons. I felt very flattered when he recognized me in his class. Two years later when I graduated, I stayed on as a member of the Parsons faculty. Even though Billy was several years my senior, we became very good friends. He had a strong, dynamic personality, a keen curiosity, and a sense of genuine caring. Always impeccably groomed, a very good-looking man, Billy was an inspiring personality.

During my years at the school, Billy shared many elements of his professional life and invited me to accompany him to decorating sites to see his works in progress. It was always a very rich experience for me. He included me in his social life and frequently invited me to parties at his apartment in Amster Yard. At the time his apartment was painted a very dark color that he called "gardenia leaf green," which he attributed to Elsie de Wolfe. Dark colors were popular in those days.

When I rented my first "proper" apartment on University Place in Greenwich Village, I painted everything white. Billy was one of my first visitors. After bounding up the three flights of stairs, he came into the apartment and began exclaiming about how much he liked the look of all white. I was stunned. At the time, no one painted rooms white. He did not comment about my having very little furniture, but

several days later he called to say that someone had given him a Louis XVI bureau plat and asked if I would like to have his Directoire writing table. This was my first piece of real furniture from a very kind and generous friend.

After five years of teaching, I opened my own interior decorating business. I was fortunate to have supportive friends, none more so than Billy. My first clients came to me through him—a distinguished couple who had just bought a garden apartment in River House, one of the most prestigious addresses in New York City. When they approached Billy about decorating the apartment, he said that he could not take on the commission and recommended me for the job. The following year when I joined the decorating staff at McMillen, Inc., and throughout my five years there, Billy remained one of my closest friends. When my life changed again and I made my best move, joining the indomitable Sister Parish in our decorating venture, Parish-Hadley, Inc., Billy was there to cheer me on.

My work was on a steady course, but Billy's life had become unsettled. Financially and emotionally insecure, he was on the brink of a dramatic change. In 1980 the time came for him to leave New York. He moved to Nantucket where he lived in a small cottage on the property of friends. I visited him only once but it was reassuring to see as we moved about the community that he had become a vital part of Nantucket. It was his new sphere of operation. Everywhere we went, he was warmly greeted and welcomed. Involved with the town library, the Congregational Church, and Meals-on-Wheels, he had drawn the curtain on his decorating career. As this book illustrates, the world never turned out the lights on Billy Baldwin. I doubt that this will ever happen.

Billy was my mentor and a great friend.

ALBERT HADLEY

# Acknowledgments

Gratitude must begin with five of the people to whom I have dedicated this book. They each had a close personal relationship with Billy Baldwin. From their unique vantage points, they made countless contributions to his story.

Deeda and Bill Blair were untiring in their efforts to provide notes and correspondence on the work that Baldwin did on their house in Georgetown, Washington, D.C. While the work was in progress and in the ensuing years the Blairs enjoyed a friendship with Baldwin. Their recounting of the times they spent with Baldwin allowed me a fuller understanding of his personality and refined manners.

Albert Hadley is the person today who best knew Baldwin. First he was Baldwin's student at Parsons School of Design; later he and Baldwin worked together as faculty members at the school; and finally they were professional colleagues in the New York world of interior decoration. Through those many years, Hadley kept files and scrapbooks on Baldwin's published work and articles relating to his career. His memories provided rare insights into Baldwin's personal life.

While Edward Lee Cave and Harry Hinson were both many years younger than Baldwin, each had close personal ties to him. Cave's reminiscences illuminated Baldwin's unyielding commitment to American interior design. Harry Hinson recalled a rare compatibility and sensibility that he and Baldwin shared in their vision of contemporary interior decoration. This was highlighted by Hinson's collection of letters from Baldwin, which he freely shared.

I am grateful to the many others who knew Baldwin and shared their memories of him: Maité Arango, Missy Bancroft, Kenneth Battelle, Rosamond Bernier, Francis Carpenter, George Davis, Murray Douglas, Hubert de Givenchy, Louise Grunwald, Mary Wells Lawrence, Walter Lees, Marguerite Littman, Susan Marcus, Victoria Meekins, Bunny Mellon, Johnny Nicholson, Andy Oates, William Paley, Jr., William Raynor, Clive Runnells, Charles Sevigny, Babs Simpson, Edward Zajac, and the late Nan Kempner.

My special thanks go to Mary Jane Pool, an editor-in-chief of *House & Garden*, who was responsible for all of the articles written under Baldwin's name and the publication of his two books, *Billy Baldwin Decorates* and *Billy Baldwin Remembers*; Coralee Leon, who was the ghostwriter for Baldwin's published work; my literary agent Helen Pratt and her husband, Charles; Kathleen Jayes, my editor; Charles Miers, my publisher; Abigail Sturges, who designed this book; John T. Hill, who provided the digital files for all of the images in the book; Jeremiah Goodman, who allowed his paintings to be used in the book; Duane Hampton, who allowed the use of the painting of the Cole Porter library by her late husband, Mark Hampton; Elizabeth Broman, Gregory Herringshaw, and Stephen Van Dyk at the Cooper-Hewitt National Design Museum, Smithsonian Institution; Leigh Monteville at Condé Nast Publications; my readers Willoughby Newton and Claudia Thomas; and Nancy Porter at Albert Hadley, Inc.

My gratitude goes to James Abbott, François de Bené, William V. Edler, III, Robert Raymond, Maury Hopson, John Peters Irelan, the late Robert Isabell, Barrie McIntyre, Mitchell Owens, and the staff of the following institutions: The Baltimore City Historical Society, The Baltimore Museum of Art, The Evergreen Museum and Library, The Gilman School, The Ladew Topiary Gardens, The Maryland Historical Society, The Metropolitan Museum of Art, The Museum of the City of New York, The New York Social Register Association, and Princeton University. If there is any person or institution that I have failed to thank, I ask your forgiveness.

Finally, to Thomas Kam Chu, my companion, for his unending support and patience I extend my most sincere appreciation.

The entrance hall of the apartment of Cole Porter at The Waldorf Towers in New York City. All of the furniture in the apartment, most of it being rare French antiques, was bought by Porter's late wife, Linda, when she and Cole had a house on the rue Monsieur in Paris before World War II. *Photo by Horst.*

# Introduction

*Billy Baldwin was unquestionably
the most influential interior designer of the twentieth century.*
Margaret Kennedy, *House Beautiful,* 1999

In 1985, two years after Billy Baldwin's death, Michael Gardine published *Billy Baldwin: An Autobiography.* Gardine, an antiques dealer, and his lover Way Bandy, the most prominent makeup artist in New York City, had provided a house on their property in Nantucket for Baldwin. He lived in this house for the last five years of his life. In his lifetime, Baldwin published two books, *Billy Baldwin Decorates* and *Billy Baldwin Remembers.* Both books are based on articles that first appeared in *House & Garden.* While the three books provide some information about Baldwin, they contain conflicting stories.

Mary Jane Pool, the revered former editor of *House & Garden,* told me that the articles attributed to Baldwin were actually written by an assistant editor, Coralee Leon. When I interviewed Leon, she told me that she based her writing on taped interviews with Baldwin. The tapes no longer exist.

Albert Hadley, Harry Hinson, and Edward Lee Cave, Baldwin's closest friends that I interviewed for this book, harbored the same resentments over the Gardine book. Each of them was adamant that Baldwin would not have said many of the things that Gardine attributed to him. They all insisted that Baldwin would not have discussed the promiscuous homosexual behavior that is described in the book. They insisted that he was a gentleman who would have never allowed these things to be published. In October 1985, the *New York Times* published a neg-ative review of the book, written by Dona Guimaraes, editor of the Home section. The editor of Gardine's book, Ray Roberts, revealed that Gardine developed the text of his book from recorded interviews with Baldwin. When Gardine died, he left a directive deny-ing anyone access to the tapes. The mystery remains: Is Gardine's book factually correct?

Another serious obstacle to obtaining information about Baldwin is the absence of any records from his decorating firm, Baldwin, Martin, & Smith, Inc. When Baldwin sold the business to Arthur Smith in 1973, he left all of the documents relating to com-missions and clients with Smith. The name of the firm was changed to Arthur E. Smith, Inc. After Smith died in 1997, all of his records, including the original Bald-win & Martin, Inc. files, were destroyed.

When Baldwin died in 1983, he left most of his pos-sessions to Gardine. Two years after Baldwin died, Gar-dine died and left his entire estate to Way Bandy. The following year Bandy died. The estates of Baldwin, Gardine, and Bandy were left jointly to two people who now live in New York City. One of these individuals was enormously helpful in my research for this book. The other one, who owns the Gardine tapes, was not. The helpful one assured me that when the contents of the estates of the three men reached him, no diaries, letters, or written documents from Baldwin were included.

Albert Hadley was Baldwin's student when Baldwin was a guest critic at Parsons School of Design. Even

*Baldwin in his one-room apartment on East Sixty-first Street in New York City. The walls were a glazed an almost-black, chocolate brown color. The St. Thomas-style sofa behind Baldwin served as his bed. Photo by Horst.*

though he was seventeen years younger than Baldwin, the two men became close friends and shared a mutual respect and admiration of their work. Hadley kept incredible scrapbooks filled with clippings and articles about Baldwin. Using Hadley's memorabilia, I was able to establish a historically accurate time line for Baldwin's life and decorating career. Harry Hinson, who owned one of the most important and highly regarded fabric and wallpaper showrooms in New York, was a good friend, and allowed me to read his collection of letters from Baldwin. Two of Baldwin's clients, Deeda Blair and Maité Arango, also shared their correspondence from Baldwin. Edward Lee Cave came to New York at an early age to study fine arts at Columbia University. After he graduated, he spent a brief time working at the interior decorating firm Parish-Hadley and later joined Sotheby's. He established the firm's first real estate office. Eventually he opened his own real estate business in New York and became one of the most elite firms that catered to high-end residential sales. While he was nearly twenty years younger than Baldwin, they were very close friends. He was enormously helpful in his reminiscences of Baldwin.

Edward Zajac, Baldwin's first decorating assistant at Baldwin & Martin, Inc., could not have been more personable but initially said that he had no details or specific information to offer. When I pressed him for stories about working with Baldwin, he responded good-naturedly, "It was all a very long time ago. I simply don't remember." Zajac did say, "With Billy everything—and I mean everything—was always nothing but the best."

Many of the available articles about Baldwin, some ostensibly containing direct quotes from him, cannot be factually correct; for example, two articles about his retirement were published within the same week in different newspapers. Each story was written by someone who interviewed him. Each contains conflicting quotations attributed to Baldwin. This kind of misinformation likely occurred for either or both of two reasons: Baldwin was not consistent in remembering and recounting events and times, and the writers exercised artistic license in their reporting.

Even Baldwin's obituaries, which appeared in newspapers all over the country, gave inaccurate accounts of his life. the *New York Times*, a "newspaper

of record," recounts that Baldwin came to the attention of his future employer, noted interior decorator Ruby Ross Wood, when he took a client shopping for fabric at Macy's in New York City. In fact, Wood became interested in Baldwin in 1930 while visiting a house he decorated near Baltimore, Maryland.

The most important documents that surfaced are transcripts of four lectures that Baldwin gave at the Cooper-Hewitt National Design Museum in May 1974. They clearly define his interior decorating philosophy. The lecture series was a fund-raising project for the Cooper-Hewitt, which had recently moved into the Andrew Carnegie mansion at Ninety-first Street and Fifth Avenue in Manhattan. Unlike the articles and books published under Baldwin's name, which may not include accurate quotes, the lectures are unassailable records of his words, ideas, and dictates. The transcripts are in the safekeeping of the Smithsonian Institution in Washington, D.C. They have been published for the first time in this book and comprise the second section of the book. Where it was necessary, I edited his spoken words for proper syntax.

This book is the last in a trilogy about three designers—Van Day Truex, Billy Baldwin, and Albert Hadley—whose careers and friendships overlapped at various stages of their lives. Writing my first two books, *Van Day Truex: The Man Who Defined Twentieth-Century Taste and Style* and *Albert Hadley: The Story of America's Preeminent Interior Designer*, and now this volume about Billy Baldwin has been a long but rewarding experience. Their stories span the waning years of the nineteenth century, the entire twentieth century, and the dawn of the twenty-first century. All of the new and exciting things that happened during this time touched the lives of Truex, Hadley, and Baldwin, and through it all they remained the best of friends.

ADAM LEWIS

*The living room of Mrs. Clive Runnells in Lake Forest, Illinois. Photo by Horst.*

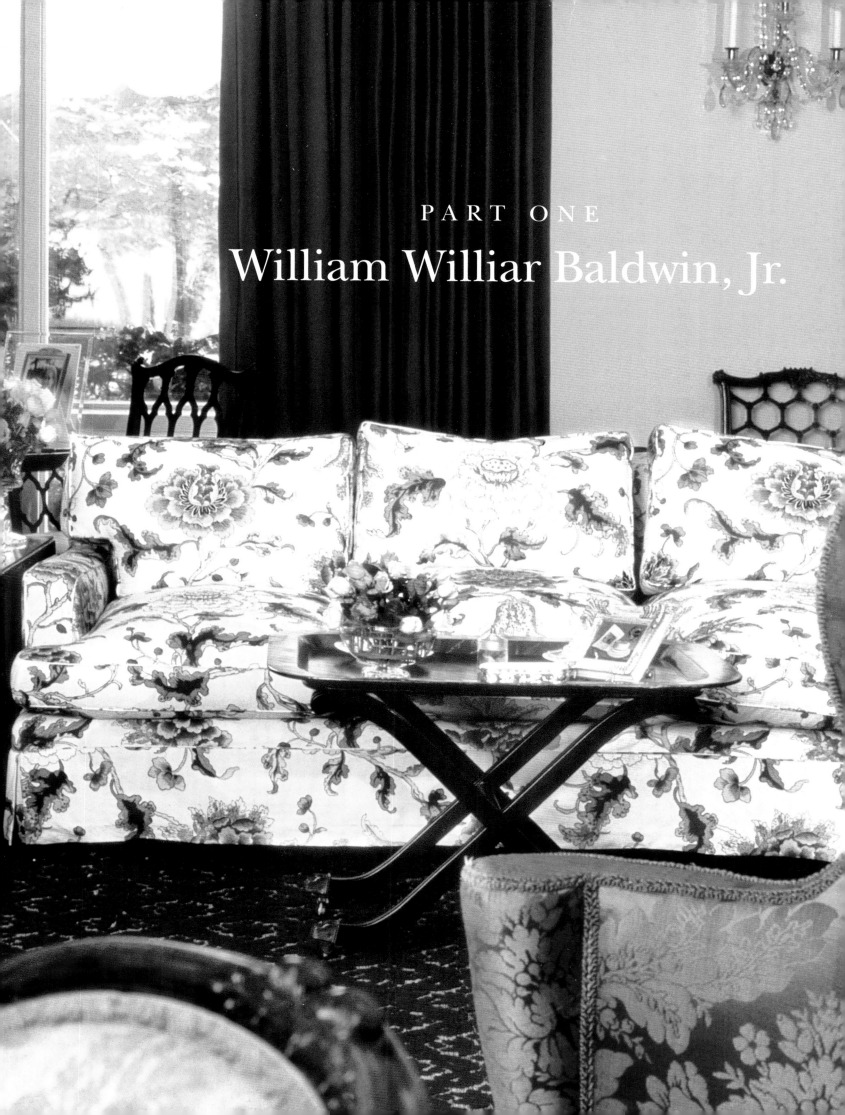

PART ONE

# William Williar Baldwin, Jr.

# The Propitious
# Telephone Call

As she put down the telephone receiver after talking with Billy Baldwin, Ruby Ross Wood recalled the cold April night in 1930, five years earlier, when she met him at the Maryland Hunt Club's annual ball. Wood and her husband, Chalmers, had spent the weekend at the home of Edith and Thomas Symington in Green Spring Valley just outside of Baltimore. When Ruby Ross Wood arrived at the Symingtons' home, she was immediately intrigued by the way the house was decorated.

She grew up in Georgia and was familiar with the propensity of wealthy southerners to fill their homes with heavy mahogany furniture. She fully expected the same thing in the Symington home, but it was quite different. The rooms in the Second Empire House did not have the cream-colored walls, white woodwork, and elaborate curtains that are common in southern houses.

The rooms were painted vibrant colors—citrus yellow, shiny magnolia-leaf green, and the brilliant red of "hunting pinks." The fabrics and trim used on the upholstered furniture, pillows, and curtains reflected the same jewel tones. There was a mix of French, English, and Italian antiques. Some of the Italian

pieces were black lacquer; others were finished in gesso with ornate gilt trim. In each room, the furniture was arranged into comfortable seating groups. Wood discovered that the bold Matisse-like palette was employed in the upstairs bedrooms and sitting rooms. She was captivated by the Symington house.

When Wood found the perfect moment for an *intime* conversation with her hostess, she asked Symington who had helped her decorate the house. Symington said that she had bought all of the furniture in Europe and that Billy Baldwin, a young interior decorator in Baltimore, worked out the color schemes and chose the fabrics. When Wood asked if she would have an opportunity to meet Baldwin, Symington told her that he would be at the ball. She mentioned that Baldwin was an extremely refined young man from an old Maryland family, and she also noted that Baldwin, who was not yet thirty, was on the guest list of every hostess in Baltimore.

Immediately after they arrived at the ball, Wood reminded Symington that she wanted to meet Baldwin. Seeking out Baldwin, Symington said that Mrs. Chalmers Wood would like for him to join them. When Baldwin arrived at the table, he remembered, "Mrs. Wood looked up at me very shyly and extended

PRECEDING PAGE

*The living room of Mr. and Mrs.
Thomas Eagan. The fabric used on the
sofas is by the Paris fabric designer
Paule Marrot. Marrot's bright floral
pattern fabrics were first imported from
France by Ruby Ross Wood. Photo by
Tom Leonard.*

RIGHT

*The library of Mr. and Mrs. Mortimer
Hall. The walls are upholstered in red
velvet. Photo by Horst.*

to me one of the most beautiful hands I think I have
ever seen. It was slender, sensitive, with perfect nails,
and she was wearing a ring set with a gigantic cabo-
chon ruby. She was round and soft looking, with a little fluff of gray hair and eyes that snapped behind the
biggest pair of horn-rimmed spectacles imaginable,
with lenses tinted faintly pink. She asked me to sit
close for a brief tête-à-tête and to tell her all about
decorating the Symington house."

Baldwin chose his words carefully, knowing that he
was talking to the leading decorator in the country.
With his usual charm, he began by saying that working with Edith Symington and her collection of
"imaginative and offbeat furniture" had been a
delight. Wood was impressed with his gracious manner
but knew full well that it was Baldwin's sensibilities
that gave the Symington house such appeal.

Not wanting to keep him from his social obliga-
tions on the dance floor, Wood congratulated
Baldwin on a job well done and said, "If we ever get
past this financial crisis, I want you to come and work
for me in New York. Seeing the Symington house
has made me realize that I need a man as my associate." She urged him to stay in touch and said that
he should drop by her office the next time he was in
the city.

In 1935, five years after their first meeting, Wood
telephoned Baldwin to come to New York for an
interview. The financial crisis was by no means over—
the conditions following the 1929 market crash were
worse than they had been in 1930 when she met Baldwin—but she could wait no longer to have him in her
employ. She was convinced that Baldwin was a genius
and had a unique flair that few decorators possess.

# Growing Up in Baltimore

It was early June 1935 when William Williar Baldwin, Jr., received the telephone call from Ruby Ross Wood asking him to come to New York City for an interview. He was then working at the decorating firm H. Chamber's Company in Baltimore and had just turned thirty-two. Since meeting Wood in 1930, Baldwin had eagerly anticipated this call. A frequent traveler to New York, he regularly visited Wood at her office at 50 East Fifty-seventh Street. She was always genuinely glad to see him and took pleasure in showing him around her gallery, as interior decorators' showrooms were called. Wood's gallery was a veritable treasure trove of antiques, objets d'art, paintings, and fabrics. Her gallery display had such style and elegance that fashion editors and photographers frequently asked permission to stage photo shoots there. To Baldwin, just being in the Ruby Ross Wood gallery was like a visit to Ali Baba's cave.

He had begun his work in interior design with the Baltimore firm of C. J. Benson & Company. After Baldwin finished his second year at Princeton in 1924, he was notified by that school that because of his poor grades, he could not return. He briefly worked at his father's insurance company, but the job was short-lived; Baldwin and his father never got along. This job was followed by a stint at the local newspaper, the *Baltimore Sun*.

In desperation, Baldwin's mother asked C. J. Benson to do her a personal favor and hire her son to work in his decorating firm. She was a longtime customer of the firm. Baldwin had no experience in retail sales and no training as a decorator, but his mother assured Benson that her son was well suited for a position in his company. She knew that he had a natural instinct for anything that had to do with interior decorating. He proved his mother right.

Benson personally oversaw Baldwin's indoctrination into the decorating business, teaching him the fine points of good workmanship in curtain making and upholstery. Baldwin regularly accompanied Benson to job sites and worked closely with him on

installations. He quickly became versed in the intricacies of the business and proved that he was a born salesman. He liked the decorating trade and was not embarrassed to be seen walking down the street carrying bolts of fabric. In a short time Benson turned over complete decorating commissions to his young liege. He told him, "Baldwin, you have it. You've got a gift that no one can learn, and no one can take it away from you."

Thinking back, Baldwin said, "When wealthy people in Baltimore wanted the very best interior decorating they went to firms in New York. I did not want to be stuck doing Chippendale forever. People in Baltimore spent an enormous amount on entertaining, food, and liquor. They didn't care how much they spent on a case of gin, but they wouldn't spend a nickel on a chair. If I had not become a New York decorator, I would still be there, weighing three hundred pounds and playing a lot of bridge." Even with these negative thoughts, Baldwin knew that the secure years in Baltimore shaped his character.

Baldwin was born on May 30, 1903, and grew up in Roland Park, the most fashionable neighborhood in Baltimore. Soon after his birth he was baptized at Grace Episcopal Church and later attended services with his mother at St. David's Episcopal Church. Except for one year, when he was fifteen, he attended the Gilman School for Boys. The year away was spent at the Westminster School for Boys in Simsbury, Connecticut. His father, who always worried about him being a sissy, thought it would be good to get him away from his mother.

Baldwin's father grew up in Baldwin, Maryland, a poor rural community just north of Baltimore. When he was in his early twenties he moved to Baltimore and opened an insurance agency. While he made a good living, Baldwin was not rich and certainly not a part of Baltimore society. This all changed in 1901 when he married Julia Bartlett. Julia's parents, Edward and Julia Bartlett, were from families that traced their roots back to colonial Connecticut. The Bartletts were one of the wealthiest families in Maryland at the time their daughter married Baldwin. The new marital status of the senior William Baldwin placed him in the Blue Book, Baltimore's social register, and elevated his financial standing.

For a short time, the newly married Baldwins lived in a modest house on Woodland Road. When their second child, Julia, known as Jule, was born they moved into a large house at 204 Goodwood Gardens, the most exclusive part of Roland Park. Julia Baldwin's money paid for the house and allowed the family to live very well. The household staff included a cook, two maids, a laundress, a personal nurse for young William and his sister, a chauffeur, and two gardeners.

William Baldwin, Sr., a handsome man, was fastidious about his grooming and attire. He spent vast sums of money on custom-made clothes and handmade English shoes, a practice that he passed on to his son. Twice each year, when the tailors from London's Savile Row came to Baltimore, Baldwin and his son were outfitted with custom suits and jackets.

When William Sr. died in 1927, Julia Baldwin immediately sold the house in Roland Park and moved into an apartment with her daughter, who was twenty-one, and her son, who was twenty-four. Billy was working at C. J. Benson at the time and had a very active social life. He was out every evening with either his smart group of young Baltimorean friends or the Valley Set, the young people so called because they lived on horse farms. Dancing was Baldwin's great pleasure. He spent a lot of time working on two committees: the Bachelors' Cotillion and the annual Junior League Follies.

As he prepared to leave Baltimore and thought back on the many privileges he had growing up there, none was more vivid than his first visit to the Cone sisters' apartments. When Baldwin was ten years old, his mother took him to visit Dr. Claribel Cone and her sister Miss Etta, who owned a great collection of twentieth-century art. The visit came about in a circuitous way. The Baldwins had a family subscription to Baltimore's Lyric Theater. Their seats were directly across the aisle from the Cones. Before performances and during intermission the Baldwins and the Cones always exchanged polite conversation.

On one occasion, when Baldwin Sr. could not attend a matinee, his wife turned in his ticket at the box office to be resold or given away. That afternoon, just as the lights were being dimmed, the Cone sisters

*Interior of the gallery of Ruby Ross Wood, Inc. In the twenties and thirties, an interior decorator's showroom was called a "gallery."* Private collection.

came down the aisle accompanied by a man (it turned out that he had been given the extra ticket). The man sat down next to the young Baldwin. When the lights came up at intermission, Julia Baldwin saw that her son was sitting next to Henri Matisse. After introductions were made, she took the opportunity to ask the Cones if she might bring her son to see their collection.

On the appointed day, Baldwin and his mother arrived for tea. That afternoon forever changed the way Baldwin saw color. He had grown up in a world that favored the soft colors of impressionist canvases. It was a world where primary colors were considered

harsh, if not vulgar. Seeing Henri Matisse's daring liberties with color and form on the walls of the Cones' apartments were a phenomenal experience for young Baldwin. He recounted, "I can remember it as if it were just yesterday. It opened a door of freedom for me." Baldwin was inspired by the intensity of Matisse's palette throughout his life, and this was reflected in his work.

The opportunity to get to know the Cone sisters was one of the many privileges that Baldwin knew he would leave behind in Baltimore. Even so, he was ready to go. Baldwin was certain that his future was in New York.

# People Who Shaped Baldwin's Life

**W**omen were the most powerful influences on Baldwin's life when he was young. His mother, whom he adored and always called "my perfect angel," doted on his every need and indulged his every whim. Like his mother, Baldwin's maternal grandmother, Julia Bartlett, never let him want for anything. From the time he was born until he started school, he had an Irish nurse, Maa, who slept in his bedroom. Baldwin once said, "I loved her almost as much as I loved my mother."

Until he was nine, the Baldwins spent their summers at The Brighton, a resort hotel in Atlantic City, New Jersey. In those years, from 1904 to 1913, the Jersey Shore was considered fashionable. On their last visit to The Brighton, Baldwin's mother felt that the clientele had changed. It was no longer a tight-knit enclave of families with whom she was comfortable. The following year she leased a cottage in the village of Siasconset on Nantucket Island, where her aunt, Ella Bartlett Robinson, had a house. For many years Ella Robinson had spent summers there with her daughter, Marguerite.

During Baldwin's first summer in Siasconset, he and Marguerite, known as Cousin Rita, developed an unusual, seemingly mystical bond. She was his mother's age; he was ten. Years later, when he moved to New York, Cousin Rita was the only member of his family with whom he maintained contact. He visited her in Siasconset every summer until her death in 1963. She encouraged Baldwin to live free of the social restraints that were imposed by the closed society of Baltimore.

Two other women in Baltimore who were not members of his family but who had great influence

*View from the reading
room into the parlor
of Evergreen House,
Baltimore, Maryland.
The teak overdoor panel
was painted by the
Mexican artist Miguel
Covarrubias. On the far
wall of the parlor is a
portrait of Alice Garrett
in Spanish dress by
Ignacio Zuloaga. Photo
by Horst.*

*The dining room
designed by Léon Bakst,
Evergreen House in
Baltimore, Maryland.
Photo by Horst.*

on Baldwin's taste and style were Alice Warder Garrett and Pauline Fairfax Potter. Alice Garrett was the wife of John M. Garrett, who before retiring to Baltimore served as ambassador to Venezuela, Argentina, and Italy. During the course of their travels the Garretts came to know some of the most important political figures and artists in the world. They regularly entertained these illustrious friends at Evergreen House, their mansion on North Charles Street in Baltimore. Evergreen House was built by members of John Garrett's family in 1878. The Gilded Age building and twenty-eight acres of gardens are now a part of Johns Hopkins University.

Although Alice Garrett was regularly in the company of government dignitaries and luminaries in the world of the arts, she considered herself a bohemian. She enjoyed painting and dancing. She was not very good at either, but this did not seem to bother her. When she entertained, which she did frequently, she gave dance recitals for her guests in a small theater that she commissioned Léon Bakst to design. Reminiscent of the sets and costumes he created for the Ballets Russes, Bakst designed a capricious performance space in what had been the gymnasium of Evergreen House. It was to this stage that Garrett summoned Baldwin to dance with her in 1925.

At the annual Baltimore Junior League Follies, Garrett saw Baldwin dance the tango and was smitten by his grace. She immediately extracted a promise that he would be her dancing partner in her theatrical productions. Baldwin became a frequent visitor to Evergreen House, where he and Garrett rehearsed and performed. She had all of his costumes custom-made and brought in dance teachers to coach them. Baldwin's most important contribution to their performances was making Garrett appear to be a better dancer than she was.

Garrett regularly entertained Baltimore society, government dignitaries, and artists, writers, and musicians, taking great delight in being the chatelaine of Evergreen House. Among the internationally known musicians invited to Evergreen House were the violinist, Efrem Zimbalist, and his wife, the soprano, Alma Gluck; the conductors Leopold Stokowski and Walter Damrosch; the lyric soprano Lucrezia Bori; and the pianist and conductor Ernest Schelling.

While Baldwin met many famous and important people at Evergreen House, the most impressive person to him was Alice Garrett. Remembering his times with her, Baldwin recalled, "The gates of Evergreen opened a whole new life for me. I knew I could never return to the life I had known before. Alice was one of the three women in my life who has meant more to me than I can ever say." The other two women were Cousin Rita and Pauline Potter.

Pauline Potter came to Baltimore in 1924, the year Baldwin began working for C. J. Benson, Inc. He was twenty-one; she was sixteen. Potter, along with Nicolas de Gunzburg, a European-born writer in New York, and Linda Porter, the wife of Cole Porter, were the epitome of exceptional taste and style to Baldwin.

Potter grew up in France. She was a young child when her father abandoned her and her mother, Gwendolyn Cary Potter, who was a drug addict and alcoholic. From then on, mother and daughter lived in a small squalid apartment in Paris. Potter's unexpected arrival in Baltimore came after her mother committed suicide. When news of his wife's tragic death reached Potter's father, he sent his sixteen-year-old daughter enough money to get to Baltimore, where she was to live with members of her mother's family. Soon after she arrived, one of her relatives, Sophie Stewart, affectionately known in Baltimore society as "Aunt Soph," invited Baldwin and some other young people to meet Potter.

Potter's manners and demeanor were French. She knew nothing about navigating Baltimore society—and she had very little interest in it. Reflecting on her time there, Potter said, "When I lived in Baltimore in the nineteen twenties and thirties, the place had an almost English atmosphere. People spoke and dreamed only of horses. Intelligence, or any display of it, was in truly bad taste."

From the hour that he met Potter at her aunt's party, Baldwin was captivated by her and became her best friend. Knowing every taboo of privileged Baltimoreans, he saw to it that Potter learned the ropes. She quickly won over the haute society with her compelling attractiveness and keen mind. She even said, "This is the most charming city in the world to make your debut. But when a girl is married, she must go to

*Celeste Marguerite Robinson, first cousin and contemporary of Baldwin's mother, Julia. She was known to Baldwin as Cousin Rita. Private collection.*

live in New York. And after that, she must live the whole rest of her life in France, married to a Frenchman." Potter succeeded on all three counts.

Her father sent her money to make a proper debut, and later, when she married, to buy her wedding dress and trousseau. She also had the income from a small trust left to her by her mother. The year she made her debut was a happy time in her life, but her marriage and the years that immediately followed were a disaster.

Even though Baldwin pleaded with her not to go through with the wedding, Potter married Fulton Leser, a raging alcoholic and a promiscuous homosexual. After a proper Episcopal Church wedding, the Lesers moved to Spain. Unable to live with Leser's

drunkenness and outrageous escapades, Potter sought a divorce and Leser returned to Baltimore to live with his mother. Potter spent the next few years in Paris and London, where she worked for the fashion designer Elsa Schiaparelli. When Potter returned to New York in 1939, Baldwin was living there and working for Ruby Ross Wood.

Encouraged by her friend Louise Macy, an editor at *Harper's Bazaar*, Potter opened her own fashion business. It was rumored that money for the venture was provided by one of her many wealthy suitors. While she had an instinct for fashion, Potter could not coordinate both operating a business and designing. Her venture failed, but it opened the way for her to work for the New York designer Hattie Carnegie.

Living the life of a courtesan, Potter's elegant lifestyle was enriched by numerous admirers. John Houston, the Hollywood movie producer, was one of the many men who showered her with gifts. She was given French impressionist paintings, as well as jewelry from Cartier, Schlumberger, and Verdura. The line of men who came to worship at Potter's altar did

*Pauline Fairfax Potter in her New York City apartment, about 1954, the year that she married Baron Philippe de Rothschild.* Photo by Louise Dahl-Wolfe.

*The living room of the apartment of Pauline Potter on Sutton Place in New York City. A Louis XV desk and Persian rug are the focal points of the room. On the mantel several pieces of Potter's collection of Chinese export porcelain are displayed.* Private collection.

not end with her suitors. A coterie of bright, talented gay men served as her acolytes. Glenway Wescott, the writer and essayist, and his partner, Monroe Wheeler, who was a curator at the Museum of Modern Art, doted on her. In like manner the fashion photographer Horst P. Horst was completely infatuated with Potter. She was his perfect model.

Basking in her new life, Potter shunned memories of her impoverished childhood and tumultuous first marriage. Baldwin was a reminder of both. While he continued to adore Potter, there is little indication that she ever returned his kindness. People who knew her said that she was uncomfortable with Baldwin's pandering. She married the Baron Philippe de Rothschild in 1954. Baldwin was never invited to their Mouton chateau in the Médoc.

But Baldwin always put her at the top of his list of people he most admired, saying she had extraordinarily creative taste, not at all derivative. He believed that everything Pauline de Rothschild touched turned to loveliness.

Dwelling on her aesthetic, he described her first apartment on Sutton Place on Manhattan's East Side. One room was white with gold-leaf moldings and the other room was an extraordinary color taken from a faded antique French silk umbrella. Some people said the room was gray; others thought it was mauve; and still others thought it was brown-green. The furniture and the pictures were beautiful. Although the apartment was tiny, there were unexpected touches that were Potter's way of making people feel loved and welcome.

Baldwin thought that one of these was her display of camellia trees. Every year about a dozen of them were delivered from a greenhouse; they were covered in the purest shade of white blossoms. Potter put them everywhere—in front of windows, in wide doorways, beside a reading chair, by a bookcase, near a bed—anywhere her guests might enjoy an extra gift of loveliness.

Baldwin always contended that Potter was without question the most charming woman he had ever known; she had charm to a degree that is unbelievable. She had the most beautiful voice, was exceedingly cultivated, and gave the impression of being a kind person, although he wasn't entirely sure she was.

Potter, Alice Garrett, his cousin Rita, his mother, and his grandmother all shaped and refined Baldwin's life in Baltimore. Other women in New York would add luster to his life, and not the least of these was Ruby Ross Wood.

# Ruby Ross Wood

During Baldwin's initial interview with Ruby Ross Wood in June 1935, she explained to him that she was offering him the job of "gallery man," as decorators' assistants were called; the job would be conditional. Even though she spent the summer months at her house Little Ipswich in Syosset, Long Island, she expected Baldwin to begin work in July. After he completed a list of assignments in his first three months, Wood said that she would evaluate his performance and decide if she would offer him a permanent job. His starting salary would be thirty-five dollars a week and she would give him the use of her apartment at 227 Park Avenue while she summered on Long Island; this included the services of her housekeeper. The housekeeper was responsible for Baldwin's breakfast and dinner, his laundry, and making sure that when he came home in the evening, the bar was stocked for him to make his martinis.

The two primary assignments that Wood gave to Baldwin were to become familiarized with the decorating resources in New York, such as the fabric and wallpaper vendors, and to visit the city's myriad antiques shops. He was to select twelve antiques that he liked and thought were important. When Wood returned in the fall, Baldwin would show her what he had selected and tell her why he had chosen each object or piece of furniture. Wood was quite knowledgeable about antiques and period furniture: she had come up through the ranks in the decorating trade.

Born into a distinguished southern family, Ruby Ross Wood (née Pope) was reared in Augusta, Georgia, where her father was a successful cotton broker. She was strong-willed, and she developed a no-nonsense attitude and a biting tongue. She spent her early years writing feature articles for southern newspapers and farm journals. In time she moved to New York City where she continued her freelance writing career. When she was in her twenties, Wood rented an apartment in Manhattan's Greenwich Village, where she quickly became a part of the bohemian community. She was not a particularly attractive woman, nor did she have any personal sense of fashion, but she was gregarious and fun-loving.

In 1907 she married her first husband, Wallace F. Goodnow. Soon after the wedding she accepted an assignment from Theodore Dreiser, editor of *The Delineator*, the leading women's magazine of the time, to be a ghostwriter for Elsie de Wolfe. Earlier

*Ruby Ross Wood*
*Photo by Jerome Zerbe.*

*Reflection of Baldwin and Louise Macy, a former editor at Harper's Bazaar. Photo by Louise Dahl-Wolfe.*

that year, de Wolfe had given a series of lectures on interior decorating at the Colony Club, an elite women's club in New York City. Dreiser wanted Wood, then writing as Ruby Ross Goodnow, to turn de Wolfe's lectures into a series of magazine articles.

The year after the series was published in *The Delineator*, Wood rewrote the material into another series of articles that was sold to the *Ladies' Home Journal*. In 1914 she reworked the articles into a book, *The House in Good Taste*, which was simultaneously published in the United States and Great Britain. That same year she published her own book, *The Honest House*, which she wrote in collaboration with the architect Rayne Adams.

The experience of working with de Wolfe's material and answering her fan mail led Wood to develop an inflated view about her knowledge of interior decorating. She temporarily set aside her writing to open The Modernist Studios, a decorating firm that specialized in the furniture that was then being produced in the avant-garde workshops in Austria and Germany. Americans weren't ready for this new look and the business failed. As Wood closed the door on her first decorating venture, a serendipitous opportunity opened for her at Wanamaker's department store in New York. Nancy McClelland, the manager of Au Quatrième, the antiques and decorating shop in Wanamaker's, offered her a job.

*Cocktail party in the apartment of James Amster, Amster Yard, New York City. Left to right: back of the butler, James Amster, Marian Hall, Ruby Ross Wood, Baldwin, William Pahlmann, Elizabeth Draper, Nancy McClelland. Photo private collection.*

When McClelland left Wanamaker's in 1918 to open her own interior decorating business, Wood succeeded her as the manager of Au Quatrième. Her new duties included shopping for antiques in England and France; selecting the accessories, fabrics, and wallpaper sold in the shop; and overseeing the quality of workmanship on all of the store's upholstered furniture and curtains.

Working under Nancy McClelland's tutelage and the rigorous demands of Rodman Wanamaker, son of the store's founder, John, gave Wood the refinement she needed. When she once again opened her own firm, she quickly became the leading interior decorator in New York City. Her success was

generated by three pivotal events. Firstly, in 1923, after sixteen years of marriage, Wood divorced her husband, Wallace Goodnow. Secondly, on New Year's Eve of the following year, she married Chalmers Wood, a wealthy stockbroker and member of the board of governors of the New York Stock Exchange. Chalmers Wood had the necessary capital to help his new wife open her own business. Thirdly, Elsie de Wolfe moved to Paris and left the field open to other competitors. Now Mrs. Chalmers Wood, known professionally as Ruby Ross Wood, had everything she needed. Her newest asset was Billy Baldwin, or Billy B. as she always called him.

# New York City

The summer that Baldwin started working for Wood she was never completely absent from the office. She came into the city two or three mornings each week to keep an eye on him. When she returned to her regular office hours in October, she followed through on assessing the assignments she had given Baldwin. In her judgment, his work was a success.

Baldwin never feared Wood's scrutiny, and he enjoyed the challenges she gave him. One of his greatest assets was confidence in his talent. This had been instilled in him by his first employer, C. J. Benson. In like manner, Wood assured him that he had passed her tests with flying colors. She raised his salary from thirty-five to one hundred dollars a week and helped him find an apartment on Sutton Place. His mother died a few weeks after he started working for Ruby Ross Wood. She left him a sizable trust fund that helped him with the expenses of decorating his apartment.

While New Yorkers considered Baltimore a backwater town, Baldwin was very much the cultivated young man when he started working for Ruby Ross Wood. He had traveled to Europe with his parents when he was quite young, and in his high school and college years he made several trips abroad. Feeling that he was a kindred spirit with his good manners and immaculate grooming, Wood nurtured a close personal relationship with Baldwin.

Chalmers Wood was frequently away on hunting trips, at equestrian events, and playing golf. Baldwin became his employer's *chevalier servant*. They worked together, ate lunch together, and frequently attended cocktail and dinner parties together. Wood was very proud of her new charge, and Baldwin delighted in her company. He always insisted that "Mrs. Wood was the best decorator ever. Her motto was 'Decorating is the art of arranging beautiful things comfortably.' She taught me the importance of the personal, of the comfortable and the new."

Wood also took great pleasure in making sure that Baldwin was properly introduced to other New York decorators and important people in the decorating and publishing trades. She was a friend of the publisher Condé Nast; Edna Woolman Chase, editor of *Vogue*; and Richardson Wright, editor of *House & Garden*. Chalmers Wood's best friend was George Palen Snow. Ruby Ross Wood nurtured a close friendship

*Brooke Marshall (later Mrs. Vincent Astor) in the dining room of her apartment on East End Avenue in New York City. Private collection.*

with his wife, Carmel Snow, the editor of *Harper's Bazaar*. Wood knew that getting Baldwin's work published was vital to his success, so she made sure that he met all of these people.

Remembering his early days with Wood, Baldwin said, "She pushed me forward, forward, forward. There were two reasons for that. She knew that she would have to work less. She also knew that the people who came into her shop, Ruby Ross Wood, Inc., would not hire me if I had not been published." Regardless of her motives, Wood wasted no time launching Baldwin. From the day he arrived in New York, she made sure that his star was in the ascent.

Recalling Manhattan in 1935, Baldwin said, "Of course I was in love with the city before I got there. When I was a student at Princeton, I often went into New York. We would go dancing in Harlem, the most attractive place you've ever known. I actually burst a blood vessel doing the Charleston at the Cotton Club. New York was glamorous then. It was enchanting. Every doorman wore white gloves and they were proud of where they worked. Don't forget there were a lot of Rolls-Royces, so even the traffic looked better. The city was clean; it looked polished and taken care of. The whole spirit was like a wonderful party. Everybody was happy and excited to be there."

To further understand Baldwin's rise, it is necessary to look beyond his talent and decorum to the nuances of his new home, New York City. The social demographics of Manhattan were dramatically different from what they are today. With the exception of Greenwich Village, there was very little social mingling of people of different ethnic and racial backgrounds.

When Baldwin moved into his first New York apartment on Sutton Place in fall of 1935, the very exclusive neighborhoods that formed his world had the feeling of a small town. His advancement was fueled by knowing people who had money and influence; and most of these people were WASPs. This was the same social milieu in which he was reared.

Baldwin's skillful networking in this closed society lay the groundwork for his success. One of Baldwin's first clients harkened back to old friends in Maryland. Another early client came to him because her sister was Chalmers Wood's godchild. Later in his career, as his reputation grew, clients came to him because they wanted the "Billy Baldwin look," but in the beginning it was all about connections.

One of Baldwin's childhood friends was Mary Clare Cottman. Her mother Mary, was one of the grandes dames of Baltimore society. When Mary Cottman heard that Baldwin was moving to New York, she wrote to her niece, Brooke Marshall, asking her to take him under her wing and make sure that he was introduced to the right people. By a strange coincidence, Ruby Ross Wood had just decorated the Marshalls' apartment on Manhattan's exclusive East End Avenue.

Soon after Baldwin arrived in the city, Brooke Marshall invited him to lunch. They quickly established a rapport. She did not forget the request from her aunt in Baltimore and took Baldwin under her wing. The other women who guided Baldwin's entrance into the inner sanctum of New York society were Helen Hull, Elsie Woodward, and Marian Hall.

Helen Hull, married to Lytle Hull, was from one of the oldest families in New York. Her first husband was Vincent Astor. Truly a leader of New York society and philanthropy, she was known as New York's First Lady of Music. She was one of the most generous supporters of the New York Philharmonic and the New York City Opera Company. Hull established the Musicians Emergency Fund along with Walter Damrosch, Yolanda Irion, Ernest Schelling, and Lucrezia Bori. Today the fund remains the steady source of income for many struggling musicians across the nation.

Hull maintained houses in New York City; Rhinecliff, New York; and Nantucket, Massachusetts. Baldwin adored her and was a frequent visitor at all of her homes. Though Hull entertained with great style, she was a very private person, consumed by her interest in music and her gardens. She enjoyed life away from the hoi polloi, quietly steering the future of organizations that interested her and the careers of promising individuals. Baldwin was one of those people.

When Baldwin talked about Helen Hull, in the same breath he always said, "Absolutely without a doubt the other grande dame of New York society, when I moved there in 1935, was Elsie Woodward. Her husband, William Woodward, Sr., was president of the Hanover

*Marian Hall. Photo by Wilbur Pippin.*

National Bank, which was founded by his family. Enormously wealthy, William Woodward owned Belair Stud, a horse farm in Collington, Maryland. Baldwin knew the Woodward family in Baltimore. The Woodwards had three daughters and one son, William Woodward, Jr.

One of the great tragedies and social scandals in New York was the fatal shooting of William Woodward, Jr., in 1955. The incident occurred at his Long Island home. During the night, his wife was awakened by the sound of what she thought was a burglar. When she opened her bedroom door and fired a pistol into the dark, she shot her husband. The tragic shooting was followed by a trial that was covered by news media all over the world. For the sake of her two grandsons, Elsie stood by her son's widow, Ann Woodward.

It was rumored that Ann had been the mistress of William Woodward, Sr., before he passed her on to his son, never dreaming that they would marry. The gossip about Ann killing her husband did not end. The cloud of suspicion hung over her for the rest of her life. Eventually Ann Woodward and her two sons committed suicide—Ann in 1975, James in 1976, and William in 1999. Through the long ordeal, Baldwin was Elsie Woodward's intimate friend and consoler. She brought him into her family and looked on him as a surrogate son thereafter. Baldwin's ties with the Woodward family extended beyond his closeness to Elsie. Years later he decorated the New York apartment and Locust Valley home of one of Elsie's grandsons, Thomas M. Bancroft, Jr.

When William Woodward, Sr., died, his wife gave a wing to the Baltimore Museum of Art for his racing paintings. This was a fitting memorial to a man who loved horses and whose ancestors had been colonial settlers in Maryland. When she made her gift to the museum, Woodward stipulated that Baldwin was to be the interior decorator of the new galleries. Today the galleries remain as Baldwin designed them. Working with the architect, Baldwin designed the interiors in a neo-Georgian style. They are fitted with William Kent–style pine paneling and furnished with eighteenth-century Chippendale and Queen Anne antiques.

Baldwin had no better friends in New York than the interior decorators Marian Hall and her busi-

*Stark Young and Baldwin in the garden of Young's Connecticut house. Private collection.*

ness partner, Diane Tate. The two women worked in the same rarified social world occupied by Ruby Ross Wood. Tate and Hall were not competitors of Wood; their firms, Tate & Hall and Ruby Ross Wood, Inc., simply served the same elite group of people.

Baldwin had enormous respect for Marian Hall's taste and style. A favorite activity was having lunch or drinks and dinner with her. When he went to her apartment he frequently had the added pleasure of seeing her good friend, Stark Young, the writer and drama critic. Young and his companion Eric Bow-

man, a prominent architect, became two of Baldwin's closest friends.

All of the women who nurtured Baldwin's success in New York fostered friendships with single men who were attractive, well mannered, and talented. Baldwin knew all of these men; he was one of them. Today such men are called "walkers" or simply "extra men." These men, with their rare talents and gifts, filled Baldwin's longings for the serendipitous. His inner circle included Nicolas de Gunzburg, Stark Young, Horst P. Horst, and Van Day Truex, plus one very special man in his life, Woodson Taulbee.

# Friends

Baldwin had six special male friends who became major influences in his personal life. Baldwin met the Baron Nicolas "Niki" de Gunzburg just months after arriving in the city, in fall 1935. Niki, as the baron was called, was an editor at *Harper's Bazaar*. Later, for a brief time, he was editor-in-chief of *Town & Country*. Eventually he became an editor at *Vogue*. Niki's parents were extremely wealthy, and he had been reared in Europe and South America. In the years before he came to America, he lived far beyond his means and spent his entire fortune on frivolities such as hosting elaborate costume balls in Paris.

He moved to New York and, through hard work and discipline, regained some financial security. He maintained an apartment in the Ritz Tower. An extraordinarily handsome man, with taste and style, he quickly found his way into New York society. Baldwin was completely smitten by him. Along with Pauline de Rothschild and Linda Porter, de Gunzburg won Baldwin's unmitigated admiration.

About de Gunzburg, Baldwin wrote, "I had the greatest respect for him. He had the best judgment about any kind of decoration of anybody I've ever

known. When you were in his two-room apartment, you expected the doors to open into an enormous hallway leading to forty-eight other rooms. He was truly extraordinary, a wonderful combination of Russian, French, and South American blood, and he spoke Russian, French, and Spanish fluently. He read like a starving man. He read everything, and without question he had a brilliant sense of humor. He was a great athlete and skied like an angel. Physically, he was dazzling."

Another man whose taste and talent captured Baldwin's unwavering attention was the writer and drama critic, Stark Young. Twenty years older than Baldwin, Young was a well-established writer when they met. For years Baldwin had been a fan of Young's novels and his writing in the *New Republic*. While Baldwin did not pursue academics beyond his second year at Princeton, he had an intellectual bent and enjoyed the company of highly educated people.

Baldwin took great delight in the fact that he and Young were both southerners. He was captivated by Young's 1934 best seller *So Red the Rose*, a novel about life in Mississippi before the Civil War. Soon after they met, Baldwin became a frequent visitor to Young's

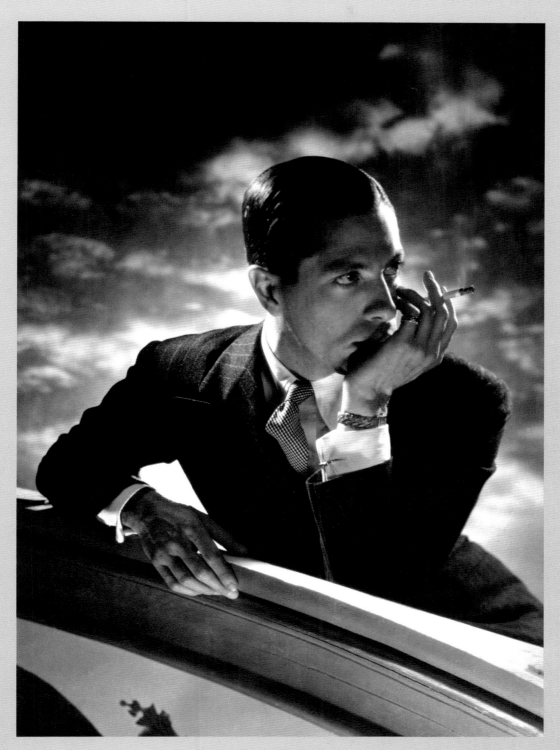

*Baron Nicolas de Gunzburg.*
*Photo by Horst.*

country house in Connecticut, and he fondly remembered Young reading his own works to his dinner guests. In 1938 Young completed a translation of Anton Chekhov's *The Seagull*, which was performed by Alfred Lunt and Lynn Fontanne. Baldwin never tired of recounting the honor he felt when he accompanied Young to opening night on Broadway.

While the photographer Horst P. Horst and Baldwin met in 1937, when they each had apartments on Sutton Place, they did not see much of each other until after the war. While Horst began his photography career in fashion at *Harper's Bazaar* and, in time, at Condé Nast, he became a highly respected photographer of interiors. The majority of Baldwin's published work was photographed by Horst.

In 1950 Horst met an Englishman named Valentine Lawford, who became his lifelong companion. Lawford began his career in the British diplomatic service. Early on, high-level officials recognized Lawford's brilliance, and it was rumored that he could have been the successor to Prime Minister Anthony Eden. Soon after World War II, Lawford was posted to New York and worked in the Security Council of the United Nations.

Lawford met Horst at a party given by Kitty and Gilbert Miller. Soon after the two men decided to live together. When Lawford moved in with Horst, he resigned from his government post. Sodomy was a crime punishable by imprisonment in England, and he knew that he could not have a relationship with Horst and work for the British government. While Horst and Lawford maintained an apartment in New York, they also had a house in Oyster Bay, Long Island. Lawford spent most of his time at the country house where he became an avid gardener and pursued a career in writing. Baldwin was a frequent visitor to their Long Island home. He considered Horst to be a genius and thought that Lawford was one of the most talented men in America.

Baldwin's closest friend in New York was Van Day Truex. Truex, a native Kansan, was born in 1904, one year after Baldwin. Truex came to New York in 1923 to attend Parsons School of Design, then known as the New York School of Fine and Applied Arts. It was the country's leading school for fashion design and interior decorating. After graduating, Truex became head of the Paris branch of Parsons. While he was there, he and the brilliant French decorator Jean-Michel Frank became close friends. Truex was made president of Parsons New York in 1942.

Truex's style was more modern than Baldwin's, and he had a more progressive outlook. Truex made Baldwin aware of modern European design trends, especially those in Paris. He also introduced Baldwin to Jean-Michel Frank. Working together in the late nineteen fifties, Baldwin and Truex took one of Frank's chair designs and reworked it into a cane chair that became a hallmark of Baldwin's interiors. In the fifties, Truex invited Baldwin to be a guest critic at Parsons—they collaborated on projects that were assigned to the students and shared in the evaluation of the finished work. In his book, *Billy Baldwin Remembers*, Baldwin devotes an entire chapter to his time at Parsons and describes the teaching experiences as one of the happiest times in his life.

After Truex left Parsons in 1953, he became the design director at Tiffany & Co. He regularly invited Baldwin to decorate one of the tables in the store's semiannual event, Tiffany Decorators' Show. When Walter Hoving, the president of Tiffany & Co., decided to open the company's first branch in San Francisco, he commissioned Baldwin and Truex to design the interiors of the new store. They later designed the interiors for the Tiffany branch stores in Chicago, Beverly Hills, and Houston.

Both men loved quality but they approached design differently. Truex was frugal; Baldwin was exuberantly extravagant. Truex preferred restraint,

FACING PAGE

*Albert Hadley.*
*Photo by Wilbur Pippin.*

ABOVE

*One of two room renderings that*
*Albert Hadley did for a class*
*taught by Baldwin at Parsons*
*School of Design in 1947.*
*The second of the two renderings*
*for the assignment is on pages*
*56–57. Private collection.*

especially in color, and adored anything beige; Baldwin loved color and glamour. Baldwin frowned on what he called "Van's colorless rooms," saying, "Someday Van is going to beige himself to death."

Even with their gibes, each man wanted to have the other's approval on anything to do with decorating or sartorial matters. Baldwin confessed, "Truex is the best-dressed man I have ever seen." He also wrote enthusiastically about Truex's cooking, the luncheons he gave in his apartment, and his "most delicious sense of humor." But Baldwin also had his peccadilloes, such as "Van thinks he has perfect taste. Whatever that means."

While de Gunzburg, Young, Horst, Lawford, and Truex were Baldwin's cherished friends, on a completely different note, for a short time, Woodson Taulbee was the most important man in his life—his lover. Baldwin always said, "It was Woody who made it possible for me to materialize my dreams."

Woodson Taulbee spent his early years in Puerto Rico. His mother, a teacher from Kentucky, went to the island in 1900 to work with disadvantaged children who lived outside of San Juan. Taulbee's father was commander of the American military installation there. In 1908, just before giving birth, Taulbee's mother returned to the United States so that he would be born on American soil. Immediately after giving birth, she took her son back to Puerto Rico where he was reared in the hills and given a modest education at home.

In his early teens, Taulbee started working in San Juan at a newspaper and magazine stand on the docks where the tourist boats came in. His good looks caught the attention of an American tourist who convinced Taulbee's parents that their son should return to the United States to have a proper education. The man, whose name is not known, took Taulbee to California. Taulbee lived there until he moved to the East Coast in 1935, when he was twenty-five years old.

Soon after Baldwin moved to New York he met Woodson Taulbee, who had gotten a job at Katzenbach & Warren, a premier supplier of fine wallpapers in the United States. According to Baldwin, "He had a very engaging smile, made friends easily, and was a successful salesman." Baldwin asked Ruby Ross Wood if he might bring Taulbee to her apartment for cocktails. Her approval on anything, especially the company he kept, was very important to Baldwin. For the same reasons, the following summer he took Taulbee to Nantucket to meet Cousin Rita.

While Taulbee and Baldwin never shared an apartment in New York City, they were inseparable until Baldwin was drafted into the army in 1942. Taulbee was exempt from military service because of a lung injury he sustained in Puerto Rico when he was a boy. After basic training, Baldwin was stationed at Walter Reed Hospital in Washington, D.C. His stint as a medical technician was a complete failure, since he fainted at the sight of blood. When Baldwin asked for a transfer to another division of the army, his commanding officer arranged for him to be honorably discharged with the proviso that he do relief work for the duration of the war.

Baldwin's first war-relief assignment was working with a supply unit that coincidentally was housed in the buildings that had been his great-grandfather's foundry, The Bartlett Hayward Company, just outside

of Baltimore. He and Taulbee would rendezvous in New York City or Washington each weekend. Due to reduction in personnel, Baldwin's job in Baltimore was short-lived. He was sent to Palm Beach, Florida, to work in the medical supplies dispensary of Ream Hospital, a government infirmary housed in The Breakers Hotel. He remained at Ream for the duration of the war.

After Baldwin was transferred to Ream Hospital, Taulbee moved to Palm Beach and took a job in the same dispensary. He and Baldwin worked together

and, for the first time, they shared an apartment. On weekends the two men frequently visited Taulbee's mother, who lived in Miami.

When the war ended, Baldwin's relationship with Taulbee took a dramatic turn. Immediately after V-J Day, on August 15, 1945, Taulbee returned to New York City. Not ready to leave Palm Beach, Baldwin accepted a job in the decorating firm of Mrs. John (Pauline, "Polly") Jessup.

Caught in the postwar spirit of victory, Palm Beach had an exuberant air and quickly resumed the old rit-

uals of opening and closing for "the season." The snowbirds, as the northerners who came south in the winter were called, arrived in Palm Beach in early December and stayed until the following March. Those four months, December through March, constituted "the season."

From April 1 until late November, the stores in Palm Beach and the homes of the snowbirds were closed. Palm Beach resembled a ghost town. Jessup and her staff used the "off-season" months to complete commissions that were to be installed

before her clients returned. During eight months of the year, there were no dances and parties; life was all about work. Baldwin found it a dismal existence.

After eighteen months, Baldwin resigned from Jessup's firm and returned to New York. Ruby Ross Wood was delighted to have him back. The war was over, restrictions on home furnishings and rationing ended, and new business was pouring in. Wood desperately needed Baldwin.

When Taulbee returned to New York the year before, he rented a room in the enormous

FACING PAGE

*A room rendering by Albert Hadley for a class taught by Baldwin at Parsons School of Design. The assignment was to use the colors in a painting that was chosen by Baldwin. Here the selected painting was "Smelt Brook Falls" by Marsden Hartley.* Private collection.

RIGHT

*"Smelt Brook Falls" by Marsden Hartley. Oil on board. 1937. 28 x 22⅞ inches.* Saint Louis Art Museum. Eliza McMillan Trust.

FOLLOWING PAGES

*Top left: Table setting for Tiffany Decorators' Show. Establishing a blue-and-white scheme, Baldwin kept the wooden surface bare and used plates with a blue cornflower design on white. The centerpiece is an arrangement of blue cornflowers with daisies and greenery. The yellow centers of the daisies are echoed in the vermeil flatware and table accessories. The cushions on the Regency chairs are covered in a cotton fabric splashed with tiny blue flowers and big yellow butterflies.*

*Bottom left: Table for Tiffany Decorators' Show. The theme of Baldwin's luxurious setting is for*

*a bachelor's dinner alone. The seventeenth-century Spanish table is set on a white goatskin rug. The dinner plate and matching bread and butter plate are sterling silver. The single-serving seedpod-shaped tureen, the owl-shaped mustard pot with matching salt and pepper shakers, and the artichoke box for cigarettes are also sterling. An elaborated Georgian-style five-light silver candelabrum dominates the table. The eight-panel screen and chair are covered in a red-and-white fabric produced by Woodson Taulbee. Beside the table is the diner's best friend—his dog, here a life-sized eighteenth-century Lowestoft hound. His bowl is a sterling porringer set on a sterling plate.*

*Right: Tiffany Decorators' Table. Serving up a "Maryland Hunt Cup Luncheon," Baldwin uses the traditional green-and-gold programs to serve as place cards. In the center of the table, he placed the 1916 Hunt Club trophy. Appliquéd on the white linen tablecloth are bright yellow lemons. The tablecloth and matching napkins are bordered in dark green. Further accenting the gold and green colors of the club are two crystal compotes filled with lemons and leaves. The yellow-lacquered bamboo chairs are English. Their seat pads are covered in a yellow-and-white paisley chintz.* All images courtesy Tiffany & Co.

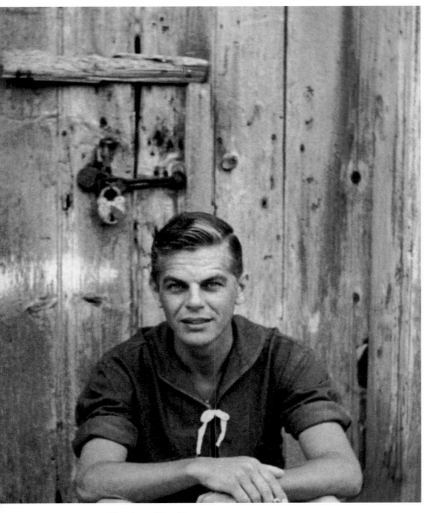

*Woodson Taulbee*
*Private collection.*

*Woodson Taulbee's apartment in New York City. Watercolor by Fabrice Moireau.*

five-bedroom apartment of Allen Porter. Porter, one of Baldwin's classmates at Princeton, then the director of the film library at the Museum of Modern Art, called his huge apartment Versailles. When Baldwin returned he inquired if Porter had an extra room for him. Porter did, but Baldwin was not prepared for what awaited him. Taulbee was no longer a paying tenant—he was sharing Porter's bedroom.

Not one to let sentiment determine the course of his future, Baldwin accepted the situation and continued a cordial relationship with Taulbee. Over the next few years, Baldwin decorated two apartments in New York for him and a vacation house that Taulbee bought in Old San Juan, Puerto Rico. In 1956, Baldwin was instrumental in helping him start his wallpaper business, Woodson Papers. The two men continued to be friends until Taulbee died in 1974.

# Interior Decoration

Billy Baldwin and Ruby Ross Wood worked together for fifteen years (from 1935 until 1950) but not continuously. Baldwin had been working with Wood for seven years when he was drafted in 1942. He spent the next four years away from New York City. This included the time he worked for Polly Jessup in Palm Beach.

When Baldwin returned to New York in 1946, Wood knew that she had terminal cancer; she immediately began turning over her clients to him. By 1948, she was very sick and spent most of her time at her home on Long Island. Baldwin managed the day-to-day operation of her business. She died in 1950 after battling lung cancer for years. Wood had trained Baldwin during the first seven years they worked together; her mark of excellence was firmly implanted in his character.

The first job that involved Baldwin when he came back to work for Wood was the Wolcott Blair House in Palm Beach. While he had nothing to do with the design of the Wolcott Blair House, his introduction to the Blair family led to commissions that came years later. In time he was asked to decorate two houses for their son, Watson Blair, and his wife Josie. He also received a commission from Josie Blair's daughter by her first marriage, Mary McFadden, the fashion designer. In an article in the *New York Times*, Mitchell Owens quotes McFadden, who said, "He [Baldwin] had a Shaker mentality. There wasn't a baroque bone in his body. Everything about Billy was meticulous, simple, and perfectly constructed."

One of Baldwin's assignments after returning to New York was working with Wood's client Harvey Ladew on his house in Monkton, Maryland. Baldwin and Ladew had been friends for many years. Ladew called his Maryland property Pleasant Valley Farm and the residence Scarff House, after the name of the family who had lived there for generations. While Ladew enjoyed being involved in the architectural plans and interior decoration of his houses, he was wise enough to know he needed professional help.

When Ladew bought Scarff House in 1929, he hired the architect James O'Conner to design the physical changes he wanted to make. Ruby Ross Wood was not the only decorator who was consulted on the interiors. Several decorators, including Elsie Cobb Wilson, Dorothy Marckwald, and Anne Urquhart, worked on Scarff House over the years.

The upstairs sitting room of Harvey Ladew's residence, Scarff House, Pleasant Valley Farm, Monkton, Maryland. This was one of the earliest applications of the color aubergine, or eggplant, on the interior walls of an American house. It may even have been the first time aubergine was used.
*Photo by Eric Kvalsvik.*

LEFT

*Two views of the living room of Baldwin's Amster Yard apartment. The walls and the fabric are pale yellow.* Photos by André Kertész.

FACING PAGE

*Baldwin in the living room of his Amster Yard apartment.* Photo by Horst.

Ladew was never happy with one person's ideas and wanted to hear several opinions before making a decision.

During the war years, from 1941–1945, all work on the house stopped. The federal government put a freeze on the manufacturing of all building supplies except those used for the war effort. Once the war was over, building and decorating supplies were available again. Baldwin and Ladew established their priorities and set about in earnest to finish Scarff House. Baldwin finished the walls in Ladew's upstairs sitting room in a highly glazed aubergine. In *Perfectly Delightful*, Christopher Weeks's biography of Ladew, he says it is believed that this was the first time a room in the United States was painted eggplant purple. The dividend for Baldwin's work on Scarff House was the close friendship he developed with Ladew. While he was much younger than Ladew and very busy with other decorating jobs, the two men frequently saw each other in New York or at Pleasant Valley Farm.

In partnership with Edward Martin, Jr., an assistant at Ruby Ross Wood, Inc., Baldwin opened his own firm in 1952. Initially, the firm was called Baldwin Interiors, Inc. In 1955, the firm's name was changed to Baldwin & Martin, Inc. He was known for using vivid primary colors and natural fabrics such as linen, wool, and cotton. He often said, "The word that almost makes me throw up is satin. Damask does make me throw up. Cotton is my life. I think cotton." This was not the case when he worked at Ruby Ross Wood, Inc.

When Baldwin was under the tutelage of Wood, he used a lot of velvet, satin, damask, and brocade, as

*Baldwin's Amster Yard apartment in 1946 showing his original "gardenia leaf" green scheme. The walls were waxed with clear butcher paste wax. All of the furnishings, with the exceptions of the rug and two sofas, are French. The lacquered screen is Korean.* Photo by Danny Wann.

*Two views of Baldwin's Amster Yard apartment. In this scheme, he has covered the walls in a cotton fabric with a large-scale print. The same fabric is used for the curtains. The lacquered French tall case clock is decorated with an intricate chinoiserie design.* Photos by Danny Wann.

well as expensive silk passementerie. That was her style and it quickly became his. This is seen in pictures of his first apartments on Sutton Place. It is even more evident in the photographs of the Amster Yard apartment, on East Forty-ninth Street, that he moved to in 1946.

At that time, the income from two family trust funds provided sufficient money for him to decorate the apartment in an elegant French manner. Like a sculptor honing and polishing stone, Baldwin changed and redecorated the apartment many times. The apartment was his decorating studio, a laboratory of sorts, where he experimented with colors and textures.

Amster Yard was a development created by interior decorator James Amster. Working with the architect Harold Sterner, the landscape designer Joseph Aacher, and the building firm Sheppard-Polk, Inc., Amster turned a couple of tenement buildings and a string of two-story working shops into a center for design and antiques. The three people who worked with Amster on the project each had offices there. Amster had his own apartment and a decorating shop, which included a showroom. There were two rental apartments, one of which was Baldwin's.

Baldwin first painted the apartment "gardenia leaf" green, the color made famous by Elsie de Wolfe. When pictures of the apartment were published in *House & Garden* in 1946, the Condé Nast office received an overwhelming number of letters praising the work. In response, Albert Kornfeld, the editor of the magazine at that time, commissioned Baldwin to write an article on color, "11 Decorating Questions Answered with Color." It received such a good response from readers that Kornfeld offered Baldwin the job of decorating editor at *House & Garden*.

When Baldwin discussed Kornfeld's proposal with Wood, her response was an emphatic "No!" Remembering her own experience of ghostwriting for Elsie de Wolfe, she told Baldwin that it was much better to do decorating than to write about it. While he took her advice, as he always did, the job offer gives a clear indication of Baldwin's growing reputation. While this was a big feather in his cap, the best thing that happened to Baldwin's decorating career in 1946 was meeting Kitty Miller. When Miller came into the gallery to discuss work for her niece Muriel (Mrs. Warren) Pershing, Wood assigned the job to Baldwin.

Warren Pershing was the son of General John J. "Black Jack" Pershing, who was a hero of World War I. Muriel and Warren Pershing were among the most popular couples in New York. They were some of the social elites who Baldwin referred to as "the most attractive people you would ever want to meet." The Pershings were pleased with Baldwin's work but, more importantly, Kitty Miller was delighted. In time, her approval reaped great rewards for Baldwin.

# Baldwin & Martin, Inc.

After Wood died on February 18, 1950, Baldwin stayed on with Chalmers Wood to assist in closing the firm and to finish any outstanding commissions. In 1952, Baldwin and Edward Martin, his assistant at Ruby Ross Wood, Inc., opened Baldwin Interiors, Inc., at 235 East Sixtieth Street. In 1955 the firm's name was changed to Baldwin & Martin, Inc. Baldwin was ready to move from the shadow of Ruby Ross Wood into the limelight. At this time, Elsie de Wolfe still had great name recognition but she was a legend. Billy Baldwin was the new star.

One of Baldwin's first clients was the fashion designer Mollie Parnis. After the drawing room he decorated for her and her husband, Leon Livingston, was published in *Vogue*, the success of Baldwin & Martin, Inc., was cemented. Many years later, after Baldwin retired, Parnis called Albert Hadley to discuss redecorating the room. He responded by assuring Parnis that Baldwin's design was perfect. He advised her to order new fabrics in the same colors and leave everything as it had been done originally.

When the young socialite Nan Kempner saw pictures of the Parnis–Livingston apartment, she knew that Baldwin was the decorator with whom she wanted to work. His use of shocking pink curtains was the kind of glamour that she adored. Kempner's life was all about being beautiful and being noticed. The apartment that Baldwin decorated for the newly married Kempners was more than a place for them to live. It was their launchpad into New York society. Baldwin and Nan Kempner became close during the time he worked on her apartment, and she became one of his most cherished friends.

Many people move from one decorator to another, but there are some clients who remain loyal to only one. Over the years, these people become more than clients—they become treasured friends. Baldwin was fortunate to have such a relationship with Kitty and Gilbert Miller. When Baldwin opened his own firm, Kitty Miller was one of the first people who made an appointment to discuss work she wanted done in her apartment. She remained his loyal client until he closed his business in 1973.

Kitty Miller was the daughter of Jules S. Bache, the New York investment banker who founded Bache & Company. When she was a child, her mother fell in love with another man and divorced her father. After

the divorce proceedings, she was reared by her father in his opulent Fifth Avenue mansion. In time, Bache left the house, along with his multimillion-dollar art collection, to the Metropolitan Museum of Art.

Miller was not a pretty child, and she went through frequent chubby periods. She also hated being Jewish. When an older Englishman named Gilbert Miller asked her to marry him, the thirty-one-year-old Kitty leapt at the chance. Gilbert Miller was a successful theatrical producer in his own right, but his wife's money launched his career to even greater heights. She was happy to do anything she could for her husband. She loved being Mrs. Gilbert Miller.

While she had little formal education, she was widely traveled and possessed a refined eye for art, architecture, interior design, and fashion. After her father died, the enormous banking fortune she inherited allowed her to indulge herself in all of the beautiful things she loved. *Vogue* editor Nicolas de Gunzburg contended that no woman in America knew more about fashion than Kitty Miller.

Miller was a leading hostess who set a standard of gracious living that few could duplicate. The guest list for her annual New Year's Eve party conferred an imprimatur of social distinction. She always had seventy for dinner and two hundred other guests who came for dancing and a midnight supper.

Baldwin met many notable people at these parties, including fashion designers Bill Blass and Hubert de Givenchy, and the jewelry designer Jean Schlumberger. These three became his close friends.

In Kitty Miller's later years she bemoaned the passing of elegant living. Once complaining about the loss of the grand manner to which she had been born, she said to an interviewer, "They're letting down the barriers. Perhaps it's necessary for the new blood, but sometimes it is not attractive." She had no one to blame but herself. Her well-publicized lifestyle was the inspiration for the social trends of the jet set, a group she deplored.

While she was a much-admired figure in New York and London, Miller's acerbic tongue could send shudders through those whose social pretensions exceeded their credentials. The only two people who could stand up to her scathing remarks were Baldwin and Margaret Case, an editor at *Vogue*. Gilbert Miller once said of his wife, "Kitty never really liked anybody." He also knew that his wife could not bear to be alone. His job as a theatrical producer meant that he kept late hours and was often away from home. To be sure that his wife had companionship, Miller paid Case's rent so that she could have an apartment in the building where he and his wife lived. The high price that Case paid for this largesse was being at Kitty Miller's beck and call. Case forfeited her personal life, never failing to respond to Miller's demands.

In addition to their fifteen-room apartment at 550 Park Avenue, the Millers had a town house in the Mayfair neighborhood of London; a fourteenth-century manor house in Sussex, England; an apartment in Paris; and a country house in Mill Neck, Long Island. It became Baldwin's responsibility to decorate and furnish all of them. This is not something he did once; the work was never-ending. As soon as work was finished in one house, there was a new project to start in another house. Baldwin frequently traveled with the Millers.

Over the years, Gilbert Miller developed a great respect for Baldwin. He commissioned Baldwin to design the sets for his play, *The Reluctant Debutante*, in 1956, and again two years later for another play, *Patate*. The *New York Times* reviews of the sets for both plays was laudatory. Unfortunately Baldwin did not belong to a theatrical union, so his name could not be mentioned in anything associated with the plays. Miller's good friend, the set designer Raymond Sovey, was given credit for Baldwin's designs. Even the files on the two plays in the archives of the New York Public Library for the Performing Arts at Lincoln Center do not mention Baldwin.

In 1968, the Millers bought an enormous Spanish mansion in Majorca, Es Molí, to be a retreat from the pressure of Gilbert Miller's hectic schedule. His health was failing and Kitty Miller told Baldwin that she wanted the house decorated and outfitted for her husband's maximum comfort. She insisted that all of the furnishings were to be made in New York and shipped to Spain. Unfortunately, Gilbert Miller died in early January 1969 and didn't see the house. Kitty

ABOVE

*Mr. and Mrs. Gilbert Miller. Private collection.*

RIGHT

*The drawing room of the apartment of Mr. and Mrs.
Gilbert Miller, Park Avenue, New York City. The
eighteenth-century painting of Don Manuel Osorio
Manrique de Zúñiga with his two cats, cage of finches,
and magpie, commonly known as "The Red Boy," by
Francisco de Goya y Lucientes was a part of Mr. Miller's
father's, Jules S. Bache, art collection. The Bache
collection of paintings, sculpture, and furniture was left
to the Metropolitan Museum of Art. According to his
bequest, Kitty Miller could borrow the painting when she
was in residence in New York City. Photo by Horst.*

*Two views of the drawing room in the apartment of Mr. and Mrs. Gilbert Miller in London's Mayfair. Photos by Horst.*

ABOVE

*The loggia of Es Molí, the residence of Mr. and Mrs. Gilbert Miller in Majorca, Spain.* Watercolor by Fabrice Moireau.

FACING PAGE

*The all-beige petit salon in the apartment of Mr. and Mrs. Gilbert Miller on Park Avenue in New York City. The paintings above the mantel and over the Louis XVI desk are by Renoir; the one near the window is by Fantin-Latour.* Photo by Horst.

*The living-dining room of the apartment of
Cole Porter at The Waldorf Towers in New
York City. The seventeenth-century
wallpaper is from the English country house
Knole, home of the Sackville family. While
filled with very fine eighteenth-century*

*French antiques, the treasure of the room is
the Parquet de Versailles floor. It is left bare
except for the three Spanish area rugs that
anchor the furniture groupings. Photo by
André Kertész.*

Miller was never happy in Majorca and donated the
property to charity. Before the house changed hands,
Horst P. Horst photographed the interiors. These
images were featured in *House & Garden*.

Gilbert Miller's death put an increased burden on
Baldwin's personal life. He had worked for the Millers
for nearly twenty years and was one of Kitty Miller's
closest friends. After her husband died, she relied
heavily on Baldwin. While this was not easy, Baldwin
had no choice but to acquiesce. From the day he
opened his own firm, her large orders provided the
infusion of cash that made the business successful.
The Kitty and Gilbert Miller account was his bread
and butter.

Soon after Baldwin opened his business, his much-
admired and dear friend, Linda Porter, was told by
her doctors that she had terminal cancer. She advised
her husband, Cole Porter, to commission Baldwin to
decorate a new apartment for himself in the Waldorf
Towers after her death. Soon after her funeral, on
May 21, 1954, Porter contacted Baldwin about the
new apartment.

Baldwin had known the Porters for years. He
greatly respected Linda Porter's decorating talent
and once said, "Linda had taste and true elegance.
Without any help from anybody, she decorated their
Paris house, their New York City apartment, and their
country house, Buxton Hill, in Williamstown, Massa-

*The bed/sitting room in Cole Porter's country house near Williamstown, Massachusetts. Baldwin's chief concern in decorating the room was comfort: good, deep chairs, functional reading lights, and a special alcove for Porter's extensive record collection.* Photo by André Kertész.

chusetts. Each place was marvelous. Linda had an extraordinary gift for using color, a natural talent for arranging furniture, and an exceptional eye for antiques. In the thirties, when she and Cole maintained a house on the rue Monsieur, she assembled a rare collection of French antiques." Cole Porter was not enthusiastic about antiques but he knew that his wife's collection must be used.

While Baldwin was fond of Cole Porter, he always said, "Cole did not have true elegance. His wife did. As his lyrics show, Cole had a clever brilliance, but every bit of his elegance came from Linda. When people complimented Cole on his luncheons or his apartment, he would say, 'You can thank Linda for that.'

Cole was terribly fastidious, he was very fond of money and luxury, and he was wildly extravagant about his clothes."

After working out the financial details of decorating the apartment, Porter left for an extended trip to Europe. His parting words were, "Have it finished when I get back, and don't you dare put a slipcover on my piano. Remember, I am Broadway." Baldwin understood the implication of this directive and captured the glamour of the Great White Way with shimmering brass bookcases fitted in a brilliant brown library. When Porter returned and walked into the apartment for the first time, he was overjoyed. He said to Baldwin, "Is all of this mine?"

The library in the apartment of Cole Porter at The Waldorf
Towers in New York City. *The famous brass bookcases,
attributed to Baldwin, were designed and fabricated by the
New York antiques dealer Frederick P. Victoria. The large
writing table is where Porter wrote all of his musical scores
even though his two pianos were in the drawing room.* Photo
by André Kertész.

FACING PAGE

The library of Cole Porter's Waldorf Towers
apartment. *Watercolor by Mark Hampton.
Courtesy of Duane Hampton.*

*Two views of the drawing room of the
investment banker and art collector
Jacques Sarlie, New York City. Photos
by André Kertész.*

The success of this apartment led to a second job for Porter. In fall 1954, Porter razed his big house, Buxton Hill, in Williamstown, Massachusetts, and moved the property's small carriage house, No Trespassing, onto the foundation. During Linda Porter's lifetime, the cottage was a place where Porter discreetly entertained gay men he invited up from New York. It also served as a retreat for him to work and compose. Baldwin was commissioned to decorate the cottage after it was moved.

At Porter's New York apartment Baldwin met Jimmy Donahue, one of the heirs to the Woolworth fortune; Donahue asked Baldwin to do some work for him on his Long Island house. He was a notorious playboy who had a reputation for hosting unsavory people, mostly gay men, at his weekend house parties. While Baldwin was openly gay, he absolutely refused to be a part of Donahue's social life, he accepted the decorating commission. The finished rooms were some of his best. A large part of the project's success was the way he used Donahue's collection of English antiques.

Pictures of the Donahue rooms reveal Baldwin's masterful use of period furniture, even though antiques were not an integral element of his style. As one of his clients said, "Billy wasn't really into antiques. If a person had antiques or wanted them, he knew how to use them, but they were not things that he cared about." He insisted that antiques must be used with comfortable upholstered furniture. When asked about antiques, he responded, "I deplore rooms so crowded with expensive vintage furniture that there's no place for people." He continued, "It's vulgar."

Baldwin's work was about simple, distinctively American design. Simplicity was always his objective. Baldwin's talent for mixing old and new, antiques and modern art, was exemplified in the apartment he decorated for the art collector and investment banker Jacques Sarlie in 1956. Pictures of the apartment were published in *Vogue*.

In the Madrid apartment he decorated for Plácido and Maité Arango, one of the wealthiest couples in Spain, in the late sixties, we again see his genius for mixing the old and the new. The apartment was in a modern building overlooking the Royal Botanical Garden. When Baldwin started work on the project he was almost seventy years old; the Arangos were in their thirties and had three small children.

Maité Arango entrusted all aspects of the project to Baldwin. She had seen his work in magazines but knew nothing about Baldwin when she first met him.

In an interview, Maité Arango recalled, "I was a young mother. I had no knowledge of decorating, but I knew what I wanted my house to look like. I wanted a very comfortable look, like a country house, nothing too formal. Billy completely understood everything I talked about. He took me on several shopping trips in New York. We selected all of the furniture, the fabrics, and the antiques. The antiques were very fine and very expensive. Billy made one trip to Madrid to see the location and the space. Since we were completely changing the existing arrangement of space, it was necessary for him to work with the architect's drawings. He did not see the actual rooms until he came for the installation."

*Two views of the drawing room in the apartment of Plácido and Maité Arango, Madrid, Spain. Most of the paintings in the room are Spanish. Some are by Joaquín Sorolla and Antoni Tàpies. Others are by the French artist Henri Michaux and Gen Paul. Photos by Howard Graff.*

"I made two other trips to New York City while the upholstered furniture and curtains were being made. When everything was complete, it was shipped to Madrid. Billy and his assistant came to Spain for the installation. Everything fit perfectly. In one room the curtains had to be shortened, but other than that, there was not one thing that wasn't perfect." Maité Arango's recollection is typical of the way his clients felt about him. As the late Mark Hampton said, "Billy Baldwin was the most beloved decorator of his time."

The dining room of the apartment of
Plácido and Maité Arango, Madrid,
Spain. On the wall facing the windows is
a contemporary tapestry by Antoni Clavé.
The great glory of the room is the

overmantel painting of Saint Thomas
by El Greco. Seldom seen in sets of twelve
are the Louis XVI armchairs covered in
leather. *Photo by Howard Graff.*

*The library of the apartment*
*of Plácido and Maité Arango,*
*Madrid, Spain. The painting over*
*the mantel is by Bernard Buffet.*
*Photo by Howard Graff.*

# Clients

Baldwin & Martin, Inc. continued to thrive into the sixties. The *New York Times* ran a story about Baldwin in 1965 with the title "Interiors by Billy Baldwin Bring Status to the Clients He Has Carefully Selected." The writer noted that most decorators gain prestige from their elite clients, but the reverse was often true with Baldwin. He then went on to list some of Baldwin's most noted clients, including Mrs. Vincent Astor, Mrs. John F. Kennedy, Mrs. Mark Littman, Mrs. William Crocker, Mrs. Henry Potter Russell, Mrs. Clive Runnells, Mrs. Ogden Phipps, Mrs. Thomas Bancroft, Jr., Mrs. Frederick Melhado (later Mrs. Henry Grunwald), Mrs. William Paley, and Mrs. T. Reed Vreeland. When Baldwin's former assistant Edward Zajac was asked about the article, he said, "Billy knew how to work for and with these people. He had no use for people who were not attractive, not amusing, and had no background."

In mid-November 1963, Baldwin received a call from Jacqueline Kennedy to discuss the interior decoration of a newly built house, Wexford, that she and the president had bought in Atoka, Virginia, near Middleburg. The following day, Baldwin went to Virginia to meet with her. Only days later, on November 22, President Kennedy was assassinated in Dallas. There was no further discussion of the Virginia house.

Three weeks after the president's death, Baldwin was summoned to Washington to work with Jacqueline Kennedy on a Georgetown house on N Street, where she planned to live with her children. Once again, she and Baldwin did not get beyond the preliminary talks. When she realized her family would be the focus of curiosity seekers and paparazzi, she knew that she and her children would have no privacy in the house. They moved to New York City as soon as a suitable apartment was found.

When she arrived in New York, Kennedy contacted Sister Parish and Albert Hadley, who had worked on the White House, about decorating her new apartment. Parish and Hadley helped her arrange the furniture in her drawing room, but they did no decorating. Several other decorators were contacted but Baldwin was never consulted.

Five years later, in 1968, Baldwin was again called for decorating advice. This time he went to Greece. Jacqueline Kennedy was now married to Aristotle

*The entrance hall of Villa La Fiorentina, residence of Mr. and Mrs. Harding Lawrence, Saint-Jean-Cap-Ferrat, France. The painting on the left wall is by Greek-American artist Theodoros Stamos. The great faux-bois doors open into the entrance hall. Photo by Horst.*

PRECEDING PAGES

*Looking into the grand salon of Villa La Fiorentina, the residence of Mr. and Mrs. Harding Lawrence, Saint-Jean-Cap-Ferrat, France. The rug was designed by David Hicks. The same pattern is used in all of the rooms on the ground floor. It is woven in a different color in each room. Photo by Horst.*

FACING PAGE

*Two views of the grand salon of Villa La Fiorentina, the residence of Mr. and Mrs. Harding Lawrence, Saint-Jean-Cap-Ferrat, France. The large lacquered coffee table and most of the other occasional tables were designed by Charles Sevigny. Photo by Horst.*

Onassis and living on the island of Scorpios. When Baldwin arrived, he found that everything in the home had been designed by Greek artisans. Jacqueline Onassis thought the furnishings were overly elaborate. She wanted Baldwin to simplify the plans and supply more traditional furniture that would be made in New York City. She also wanted it completed by Christmas, then sixty days away.

Aristotle Onassis concurred with everything his wife wanted and gave Baldwin carte blanche to do the job. On his return to New York, Baldwin set about having the upholstered furniture and

A small second-floor alcove in Villa La Fiorentina, the residence of Mr. and Mrs. Harding Lawrence, Saint-Jean-Cap-Ferrat, France. An eighteenth-century desk faces a low yellow table taken from a design by Jean-Michel Frank. Above each is a drawing by Jack Youngerman. On the back wall is a large painting by Cleve Gray. Both of the artists are American. *Photo by Horst*

The library in Villa La Fiorentina, the residence of Mr. and Mrs. Harding Lawrence, Saint-Jean-Cap-Ferrat, France. The boiserie is glazed the color of natural straw. The color is repeated in the linen curtains. All of the furniture is upholstered in linen printed with green and white flowers. On the fireplace wall is a series of collages by the American artist Anne Ryan. *Photo by Horst.*

*The dining room of Villa La Fiorentina, the residence of Mr. and Mrs. Harding Lawrence, Saint-Jean-Cap-Ferrat, France. Three round tables like the one seen here were always set for four for dinner. Photo by Horst.*

Mr. Harding Lawrence's study in the Villa La Fiorentina, Saint-Jean-Cap-Ferrat, France. Baldwin described the color of the wall and curtains as the color of "hot biscuits." The sofa is flanked by two Sheraton chairs which Baldwin described as "the color of English riding boots." The pillows on the sofa were made from Indian saris. The Persian paintings are the only exceptions to the Lawrences' insistence that all of the art in the villa be by American artists. *Photo by Horst.*

*The foyer that leads into the library at Villa La Fiorentina, the residence of Mr. and Mrs. Harding Lawrence, Saint-Jean-Cap-Ferrat, France. The large painting is by the American artist Thomas Phelps Stokes.*
Watercolor by Fabrice Moireau.

curtains made and shipped to Greece in less than two months. He did not return to Scorpios for the installation and he never saw the house again.

Jacqueline Onassis lived in Greece for a very short time and soon returned to New York City. In 1975, Aristotle Onassis filed for divorce, but he died before it was finalized. She reached a twenty-million-dollar settlement with the executors of Onassis's estate. For the first time in her life, she could have decorated any house or apartment that she chose exactly as she pleased. Unfortunately, Baldwin had closed his business two years earlier.

Remembering their times together, Baldwin said, "I'm devoted to Jackie. The last time I saw her, Bunny Mellon picked me up in her plane, and we flew to Martha's Vineyard and had lunch at her new house. I never thought that Jackie was really elegant. She's an intellectual. Even more, she is a witch—she really has magic. One of her witch's qualities is, whenever you see her on the street she greets you with the wildest enthusiasm, and makes you believe you're the best friend in her life."

Two of Baldwin's clients, Mary Wells and Harding Lawrence, were so busy with their hugely successful careers that they refused to take time to look at colors, fabric samples, or to make furniture selections. They simply told Baldwin to do the work and call them when it was finished. This happened with their

house in Dallas, their ranch in Arizona, their apartment in New York, and their villa, La Fiorentina, on the Côte d'Azur.

Mary Wells Lawrence was president and chairman of Wells Rich Greene, the advertising firm she started in 1966. Within months after she opened her agency, the firm was billing over thirty million dollars in business. Five years later the figure was over one hundred million dollars, and she was the highest paid woman in the United States. She married Harding Lawrence, one of her clients and the founder and CEO of Dallas-based Braniff Airlines, in 1967.

Talking about her experiences with Baldwin in an interview, Mary Lawrence said, "Billy liked working for us because I gave him complete control. He was very bossy, an awful lot of fun, articulate and extremely kind. He was also very naughty. Living in rooms that he decorated is like going to some wonderful school. He gave me different lives to lead. Billy put a house together with expectations of how I would live in it. He gave me a dining room where I could have a large party, but when the party was over, the space became a living room, an intimate sitting room. The way he designed my dressing rooms taught me how to hang up my clothes. He was quite simply a genius."

She continued, "When Billy oversaw the installation of a house, everything arrived on the same day.

RIGHT

*The drawing room of the residence of Ambassador and Mrs. William McCormick Blair, Jr., Georgetown, Washington, D.C.* Photo by Horst.

Seeing him work was like watching someone direct an operetta. He instantly placed everything in the right spot; there was no hesitating at all. By the end of the day all of the furniture and accessories were miraculously in place. There was never any trial and error." He also decorated the offices of Wells Rich Green in New York City.

While each of the four residences that Baldwin decorated for the Lawrences was a triumph, the house at Saint-Jean-Cap-Ferrat on the Côte d'Azur was unquestionably the most spectacular. The Palladian-style villa is built on a point of land that juts out into the water; on one side is the Mediterranean and on the other is Beaulieu Bay. It is one of the most magnificent locations on the Riviera. When the Lawrences bought La Fiorentina, it was owned by one of Baldwin's friends, Rory Cameron. He and his mother bought the house in 1939. After World War II, Cameron did a masterful job of reworking the villa's structure and decorating it. When Cameron turned over his prized creation to the Lawrences, he was living only a few hundred feet away in Le Clos, a dower house on the property.

Baldwin was not fluent in French, so he retained the services of Charles Sevigny, an interior decorator in Paris, to help carry out his plans. Sevigny, an American expatriate, had graduated from Parsons School of Design and was a close friend of Van Day Truex.

While the work was being done on the villa, Baldwin and Sevigny stayed with Cameron at Le Clos. Truex, who was then living in the south of France, frequently came for visits. With four opinionated arbiters of taste on site, Baldwin's plans for the villa could have become a design collaborative. Although Baldwin listened to the ideas of these three much-admired friends, he did exactly what he wanted.

Baldwin transformed every room in the house, moving away from the former owners' old-world heaviness. His no-nonsense, spare aesthetic was most evident in the blue salon, which is the heart of the villa. The walls were painted white and all of the upholstered furniture was covered in blue linen. The lamps and the garniture on the marble mantel were blue-and-white Chinese porcelain. The room and everything in it reflected the sky and the sea that were beyond the French doors opening on to the terrace. Remembering the work, Baldwin said, "They did not want to see one thing. I was told to buy everything. Mary and Harding did not come to the villa until it was completely finished."

Many of Baldwin's clients also figured prominently in his social life. He called them "The Stars in My Crown." These "stars" included Deeda Blair, the wife of Ambassador William McCormick Blair; Louise Grunwald, wife of Ambassador Henry Grunwald; Bunny Mellon, who was married to Paul Mellon; Babe Paley, the wife of William Paley, the founder and chairman of CBS; Mrs. T. Reed "Diana" Vreeland, the infamous editor of *Vogue*; Mrs. Clive Runnells who had houses in Hobe Sound, Florida, and Lake Forest, Illinois; and New York socialite Mrs. Thomas "Missy" Bancroft, Jr.

Baldwin's last commission before closing his business was for Tom and Missy Bancroft. He fondly remembered the master bedroom suite that they added to what he already thought was a wonderful country house, Thanksgiving, on Long Island. Based on his suggestion, the Bancrofts hired the architect that Baldwin worked with when he decorated Cole Porter's house in Massachusetts.

Baldwin created a family room on the first floor of the new addition. He recalled, "It was a sunny, sunny room with white walls and enormous windows. Most of the windows opened onto the terrace. I covered most of the furniture in East Indian cotton slipcovers. This room and the master bedroom, on the second floor, were all about light, light, light. These two rooms were the very last things that I did at the end of my lengthy career."

He continued, "While I enjoyed the work on the new wing of Tom and Missy's house, I also loved working on the old part of the house. The structural details—the bones—were superb. The formal living room was brilliantly lit, not from lamps but with natural light. It was wonderful to sit in. It didn't matter if there were three people or eighteen, the room was extraordinary. All of the furniture had come from previous generations and was simply re-covered. I

ABOVE

*The staircase in the residence of Ambassador and Mrs. William McCormick Blair, Jr., in Georgetown, Washington, D.C.* Photo by Horst.

RIGHT

*Mrs. Blair's eighteenth-century French bed in her home in Georgetown, Washington, D.C.* Photo by Horst.

112 *Clients*

*The library in Thanksgiving,*
*the country house of Mr. and Mrs.*
*Thomas Bancroft, Jr.* Photo by Horst.

think this is what gives a room atmosphere. Old furniture with good lines, not necessarily antiques, brings a feeling of permanence that brand-new things don't have. I loved using their old family pieces with a contemporary Moroccan rug." Baldwin's ties with the Bancrofts went back to Tom's grandmother, Elsie Woodward, who had warmly welcomed him to New York City forty years earlier.

When Baldwin was commissioned to decorate Ambassador and Mrs. William Blair's large Georgian-style house, they were important figures in Washington, D.C. Working on the Blairs' house was the beginning of a treasured friendship between Baldwin and his clients.

Recalling Deeda Blair, Baldwin said, "I have never worked with anyone who was more in love with her house. Everything, every single flower, was done by her. She never stopped doing little things here and there. She completely understood the personal in decorating. Deeda Blair never rushed out and bought anything. She waited and waited and waited for what was right in the place where she placed it. Once we had completely finished a room and she found two Chinese panels that were installed on either side of the chimneypiece. They were absolutely perfect. I promise you that there was not one thing in her

*The sunroom in Thanksgiving, the
country house of Mr. and Mrs.
Thomas Bancroft, Jr.* Photo by Horst.

*The living room in Thanksgiving, the
country house of Mr. and Mrs.
Thomas Bancroft, Jr.* Photo by Horst.

whole house—every single object, I promise you—
that she did not choose because she loved and
cherished it. There was not a chance that any of her
things would ever get dusty. She was forever rear-
ranging them."

Remembering her long relationship with Baldwin,
Deeda Blair said, "Two words describe Billy, 'impec-
cable' and 'graceful.' It was an enchanting experi-

ence to be in his presence." Today the Blairs live in New York City. Many of the things that Baldwin did for their Washington house are now very much at home in their New York apartment.

When Baldwin first met Louise Grunwald she had recently been divorced. Then Louise Savitt, she was starting a new job at *Vogue*. Diana Vreeland called Baldwin and asked him for a big favor. She wanted

him to decorate Louise Savitt's apartment at no charge and to get whatever she needed at his decorator's discount. Baldwin adored Vreeland and happily accepted. He and Savitt became fast friends. When she married Frederick Melhado, Baldwin again came to her aid. Melhado's apartment, where the newly married couple were to live, had recently been decorated by Albert Hadley. It became Baldwin's job

ABOVE

*Mrs. T. Reed (Diana) Vreeland's desk in her apartment designed, at her request, to look like "a garden in hell."* Photo by Richard Champion.

RIGHT

*The living room in the apartment of Mr. and Mrs. T. Reed Vreeland at 550 Park Avenue in New York City.* Photo by Richard Champion.

*The dining alcove in the apartment of Mr. and Mrs. T. Reed Vreeland, 550 Park Avenue, New York City.* Photo by Richard Champion.

*Mrs. Vreeland's bedroom in her Park Avenue apartment.* Photo by Richard Champion.

FACING PAGE

*The living room in the suite of Mr. and Mrs. William Paley at the St. Regis Hotel in New York City. Photo by Louis H. Frohman.*

to integrate her furniture and accessories, mostly things from her mother, into the Hadley scheme. Doing this kind of very personal work endeared Baldwin to his friends.

Baldwin first met Bunny and Paul Mellon in 1961 when he attended their daughter Eliza's debutante party in Upperville, Virginia. Paul Mellon was the only son of Andrew W. Mellon, who founded the Aluminum Company of America (ALCOA), the Gulf Oil Corporation, the Union Trust Company, and the Pittsburgh Iron and Coal Company. He also endowed the National Gallery of Art in Washington and appointed his son, Paul, to oversee the building of the museum.

Bunny Mellon first called Baldwin to hire him to work on her house in the Caribbean, at the Mill Reef Club in Antigua. The cotton and linen fabrics and straw-covered furniture that Baldwin preferred were perfect for the island climate. Even though she had vast wealth, Mellon loved simple fabrics and hated anything that even bordered on being grand. Over the next ten years, Baldwin did work for Mellon in New York City; Upperville, Virginia; and Cape Cod, Massachusetts. The Mellons were very private people and would not allow any of Baldwin's work in their homes to be published. None of the rooms he did for them were photographed.

Remembering his years working with Mrs. Mellon, Baldwin said, "Bunny has true elegance in terms of taste and decoration. She's a great horticulturist and has a rare gift for architecture. In houses she has the most outstanding taste of anybody in this country.

Her house in Antigua is a dream, absolutely right for the island. I find in so many resorts, the ugliest house is owned by the richest man. There's often a vulgarity about having too much money, because there's no restraint. But you're never aware of Bunny Mellon's money in anything."

When asked about Baldwin for this book, Mrs. Mellon replied in a letter, "It's always been my instinct not to give an interview about a friend, and Billy was one of my best-loved friends. We could spend hours crowded with new and spontaneous ideas. His taste was unique and ahead of his time."

The letter continues, "Often I watched him waiting to cross Lexington Avenue on his way back from the D & D [Designers & Decorators] Building [in New York City]—the street was always crowded with people on the run and heavy moving traffic. Billy, half the size of anyone, stood erect, beautifully dressed. With or without a smile, you felt he was in control of the scene and those about him. This was his natural presence. Billy Baldwin lived for many years in Nantucket before he died there, and left us with admiration for his everlasting charm and honesty."

The only thing more colorful than the apartment Baldwin created for Diana Vreeland was Vreeland herself. Her long career in New York began as fashion editor at *Harper's Bazaar*. She was there for twenty-five years. Her subsequent work years were spent at *Vogue*, where she was editor-in-chief for nine years. In 1971 she became a special consultant to the Costume Institute at the Metropolitan Museum of Art. With all of the glamorous perks

*The living room of the suite of
Mr. and Mrs. William Paley at the
St. Regis Hotel in New York City.*
Photo by Louis H. Frohman.

*Detail of the Venetian mirror in
the suite of Mr. and Mrs. William
Paley at the St. Regis Hotel in
New York City.* Photo by Horst.

*Two views of the living room in the home of Mrs. Clive Runnells, Casa Contenta in Hobe Sound, Florida. The red end tables are Chinese hatboxes. Photo by Horst.*

that came with her jobs, Diana Vreeland never had much money. She and her husband lived modestly but with enormous style. In 1955 they moved into a small apartment at 550 Park Avenue, but it was far from the grand spaces that one associates with such a prestigious address. The Vreeland apartment was small and poorly laid out. The help of a skillful decorator was required. In 1957 Baldwin came to the rescue of his close friend.

Vreeland told Baldwin that the budget was small and that she wanted the apartment "to look like a garden—not just any garden, but a garden in hell." Baldwin's challenge was to find inexpensive fabrics that did not look cheap. He was dealing with one of the great tastemakers of the world who happened to

have very little money.

Baldwin solved the problem on a trip to Madrid. He found the material that he used at the Spanish fabric house Gastón y Daniela. The cotton fabric was predominantly red and printed with a black-and-white floral pattern. The design was similar to the very expensive fabrics produced by the famous French firm Braquenié. The Spanish fabric was not only the perfect color and design, it was also the right price at less than two dollars per yard. Baldwin did not wait for Vreeland's approval. He bought all of the fabric in stock and had it shipped to New York. He ordered the same fabric in blue for the bedroom.

The "garden in hell" was neither remotely hellish nor particularly horticultural. Aside from the flamboyant

*The living room in the residence of Mrs. Clive Runnells in Lake Forest, Illinois. The paintings on either side of the mirror at by Canaletto. Photo by Horst.*

scarlet-flowered cotton fabric on the walls and curtains of the living room, everything else in the room was red: red carpet, red-lacquered doors, red closet linings and picture frames. When Richard Campion came to take pictures of the apartment, Vreeland said, "If you can photograph this place, the Sistine Chapel ceiling will be a cinch." She then added, "It was done in 1957, and even then it was a period piece." Her courage to be original gave Baldwin the chance to produce one of the most photographed apartments in the history of American interior design.

Spaces that would have been far easier to work with than those of the Vreeland apartment were the myriad rooms that Baldwin created for Babe and William Paley in New York City and on Long Island, and for Mary Runnells in Lake Forest and Hobe Sound.

The walls of the drawing room that Baldwin created for the Paleys in their suite at the St. Regis Hotel were hung with a shirred brown paisley print cotton. It was an effect quite unlike his characteristic crisp, hard-edged look. Later, he used the same shirred-fabric look in an apartment he decorated for the writer Speed Lamkin and again in the bedroom/sitting room he decorated for Nan and Thomas Kempner.

In the Paley apartment the furniture was covered in very light colors or the same paisley that was used on the walls. All of the upholstered pieces had the lines and details of Second Empire furniture. Baldwin was one of the first decorators in this country to emulate the look of Madeleine Castaing at a time when most Americans did not know what Second Empire furniture was.

On the floor of the Paley living room Baldwin used a multicolored needlepoint rug, and from the ceiling of the living room he hung a Venetian chandelier that featured a pair of blackamoors and a clock of Brighton Pavilion chinoiserie. The finished room was a perfect reflection of Babe Paley's glamour and great beauty. On several occasions Horst P. Horst photographed her standing before her Beaux-Arts mantel of bronze doré and marble. When Baldwin wrote a chapter for *The Finest Rooms by America's Great Decorators,* he elected to feature the Paley drawing room. He went on to decorate the Paley's apartment at 820 Fifth Avenue and the house on their vast estate, Kiluna, in Manhasset, Long Island.

Mary Runnells was one of Baldwin's "A-list" clients. He decorated houses for her in Florida and Illinois. Recalling the work he did on her Lake Forest house, Baldwin said, "We worked on the house for more than twenty years but we never changed the basic floor plan. Mrs. Runnells was an extraordinary woman with absolutely wonderful taste. She knew exactly what she wanted and she could afford the best. In her travels, and she traveled a lot, if she saw a chair or table that she liked and it was superior to the one we had already bought, she would buy it. She loved English furniture. Because all of her things were truly museum quality, I am sure that after her death they went to the Chicago Art Institute."

Continuing his recollection of her he said, "Everybody has a strong idea of what elegance is, of what style is, and with each person it's always completely different. Elegance is definitely inborn. It's a quality way beyond chic. It's the rarest of qualities in people, in decoration, in life. It's not possible to learn it the way you can learn style. Mary Runnells had true elegance."

Not only did Baldwin do some of his most important work in the sixties, he also began writing a series of articles for *House & Garden* that further enhanced his reputation as the dean of American decorating. In 1972 these articles were published under the title *Billy Baldwin Decorates.* The book was so successful that it was reprinted twice in 1973, and it insured Baldwin's reputation far beyond New York City and the narrow enclaves of the social elite. Billy Baldwin became a household name in America and he became synonymous with interior decoration throughout the world.

# Commercial Contracts

Baldwin did little commercial decorating during his career, but two jobs completed in the mid-sixties established his reputation for being adept at handling large-scale projects. He worked on The Round Hill Club in Greenwich, Connecticut, and Kenneth Battelle's ladies' hairdressing salon, Kenneth, that occupied a limestone house on East Fifty-fourth Street between Fifth and Madison Avenues.

According to Battelle, when he contacted Baldwin and asked him to consider the project, Baldwin refused. He said he was not interested in doing commercial work and would not even consider an initial interview. When Battelle shared this with one of his clients, who was also one of Baldwin's clients, the woman said she would see what she could do. She contacted Baldwin and convinced him to at least meet with Battelle and then make up his mind.

Baldwin and Battelle hit it off immediately, and the project was a success for both men. Kenneth was decorated in a style reminiscent of "Brighton Pavilion," employing the use of fabrics in exotic patterns. Glossy lacquer in bright red, yellow, and white was used throughout the rooms. The elevators were draped with fabric to resemble tents. When the salon was completed, it received international publicity including an extensive article in *Vogue* accompanied by Henry Koehler drawings of the salon and its famous clients.

Baldwin hated being called an interior designer. He thought it was pretentious and connoted an architectural expertise that most decorators didn't have. He did not have this training and always relied on professional architects. Baldwin wanted to be called an interior decorator. He insisted that decorating was what he did, and he was proud of his work.

In the early seventies Baldwin signed a licensing agreement with Luten Clarey Stern, Inc., allowing the company to market a line of furniture. Everything in the Billy Baldwin Collection was designed by one of the partners of LCS, William Goldsmith. Using the Billy Baldwin name worked well for LCS and the collection was a great success. Some of the pieces that Goldsmith designed are still being marketed.

The brass bookcases, or étagères, that Baldwin reportedly designed for Cole Porter's library were in fact designed by the New York antiques dealer Frederick P. Victoria and made in his workrooms. Victoria's son, Anthony, retains his father's original

PRECEDING PAGE

*View into Kenneth, 19 East Fifty-fourth Street, New York City. The entire building that housed the salon was completely destroyed by fire in 1990.* Private collection.

ABOVE

*Detail of a wall light and wallpaper at Kenneth on East Fifty-fourth Street in New York City.* Private collection.

RIGHT

*A view of the styling room of Kenneth on East Fifty-fourth Street in New York City.* Private collection.

ABOVE

*Detail of two wallpapers and a table lamp.* Private collection.

FACING PAGE

*A drawing of the styling room by Henry Koehler, Kenneth on East Fifty-fourth Street in New York City . The entire salon was decorated in the spirit of the great pleasure palace "Brighton Pavilion."*

136   *Commercial Contracts*

FACING PAGE
*Room display at the Luten Clarey Stern, Inc. showroom, New York City. The red-and-white fabric and the straw-covered furniture were a part of the firm's Billy Baldwin Collection.* Photo by Norman McGrath.

sketches, working drawings, and specifications for the bookcases. Anthony Victoria also has a photograph of the rolling tea cart that inspired his father's design. The Billy Baldwin–Cole Porter bookcases remain in production.

In the fifties, Baldwin worked with Van Day Truex to decorate the showrooms of Tiffany & Co. The two men produced the chairs that were used in the newly decorated spaces. The cane chairs were based on a design by Jean-Michel Frank and handcrafted by Bielecky Brothers, Inc., in its Long Island City workrooms. These chairs were not exclusive to Tiffany—Baldwin also used them in other work—which meant they were frequently seen in decorating magazines. The chairs are still made and marketed by Bielecky as "Billy Baldwin" chairs.

The famous slipper chair, also attributed to Baldwin, was first seen in houses decorated by Ruby Ross Wood and made in her workrooms. When Baldwin gave a series of lectures at the Cooper-Hewitt National Design Museum in 1974, he said that Ruby Ross Wood was completely responsible for the design of the chair. His contribution to the commercial success of the chairs was making them much smaller than Wood's original.

In the world of decorating and design, Baldwin's greatest fan, for a time, was the English decorator and designer, David Hicks. Hicks considered Baldwin and John Fowler, Baldwin's English counterpart, the two greatest decorators of the twentieth century.

In summer 1960, while traveling in the south of France, Hicks met Van Day Truex. In the course of their conversations, Hicks said that he would like to meet Baldwin. Truex did not hesitate to write his friend and ask him to welcome Hicks to New York City. Hicks made his first trip to America that fall and he called on Baldwin.

The two men became fast friends, though Baldwin was twenty years older than Hicks. Baldwin introduced Hicks to everyone of importance in the New York decorating community. He also took Hicks to the showrooms of the leading suppliers of fabrics, wall coverings, floor coverings, lighting fixtures, and architectural hardware. Exposure to these products had a dramatic effect on the young designer. They were yet to be marketed in postwar England and were barely known in the London design world.

Baldwin and Hicks shared a mutual admiration for years and made a concerted effort to seek out each other's company. Baldwin wrote, "David Hicks revolutionized the floors of the world with his geometric carpets." He used Hicks-designed carpets many times in his commissions. When Baldwin decorated La Fiorentina for Mary Wells and Harding Lawrence, he used David Hicks rugs throughout the ground floor.

Ego reared its ugly head and the friendship soured. In 1971 Hicks dedicated his fourth book, *David Hicks on Decoration–with Fabrics,* to Baldwin and Fowler. In Baldwin's thank-you note to Hicks, he wrote about "being proud of him." Hicks thought this was patronizing and the two men argued; the rift between them was never healed. In Ashley Hicks's

first book about his father, Hicks is quoted as saying, "Billy Baldwin, that pompous old bore, didn't have a shred of originality in his whole body." Fortunately no one cared what Hicks thought of Baldwin—least of all Baldwin. His reputation and success were assured. He was the most celebrated decorator in America and no one could take that away from him. He liked being the toast of the town.

Baldwin never tired of dressing up in his tuxedo and always enjoyed the social whirl of New York. He loved big parties with hundreds of guests as much as intimate dinner parties with six or eight people. It didn't really matter, just as long as everyone was attractive and had something to say. While he had many memorable evenings out, there is little doubt that two of Baldwin's most unforgettable nights were the Truman Capote Black and White Ball in 1966 and the Metropolitan Museum of Art Centennial Celebration in 1970.

Capote's party at the Plaza Hotel was given in honor of Katharine Graham, the publisher of *The Washington Post.* Many New Yorkers remember it as the city's last great private party. Assembled under one roof were the most noted politicians in the country, titans of business, as well as writers, artists, actors, and socialites. Without question it was the most highly publicized party in the history of the Plaza. Everyone came dressed in black and white and wore original masks. Halston, the most celebrated American fashion designer at the time, charged thousands of dollars for the masks he created for some of the revelers. Gene Moore, the window designer at Tiffany, made matching silver masks for Baldwin and Van Day Truex. They arrived as a pair of unicorns.

As a part of the Metropolitan Museum's Centennial Celebration, four interior design firms, Baldwin & Martin, Parish-Hadley, McMillen, and Burge-Donghia, were each asked to decorate a room in the museum for the party. On the day of the big event, the museum offered free admission, free soft drinks and coffee, and slices of birthday cake. Admission to the evening gala was by invitation only. Every notable person in the city of New York was there.

To accommodate the broad spectrum of taste, there were four dances going on in four separate

*Fabric from the Billy Baldwin Collection produced by Woodson Taulbee for Woodson Papers, Inc. Watercolor by Fabrice Moireau.*

141

rooms of the museum. Each room was decorated to celebrate an important year in the life of the museum: 1870, 1911, 1930, and 1970. The guests feasted on pheasant pie and sipped champagne in the Viennese ballroom created by Albert Hadley in the Armor Court and had their dessert in the belle epoque room decorated by McMillen in the Blumenthal Patio. A roof-garden supper club typical of the thirties was created by Angelo Donghia in the Egyptian Sculpture Court.

The young set was in the museum's Fountain Restaurant where Baldwin created a contemporary discotheque. He transformed the space, originally designed by Dorothy Draper, into what *Newsweek* magazine called "a plush turn-of-the-century Parisian brothel rather than a boîte de nuit." Under Baldwin's guiding hand, his old friend Woodson Taulbee created 3,000 yards of gold-encrusted fabric, reminiscent of Gustav Klimt, that covered every square inch of the room, including the chandeliers. While all of the decorating schemes were successful and beautiful, the scale of Baldwin's room was by far the most dramatic. The smallest man at the party made the biggest splash.

In the early sixties, in the midst of his glamorous life, Baldwin suffered a humiliation that plagued him for as long as he lived. Due to errors in his personal accounting, none of them caused by Baldwin, he was indicted on a federal income tax evasion charge. No

one believed that Baldwin was guilty. None of his clients and friends thought this, but their sympathy and support did not ameliorate his embarrassment.

Kitty Miller paid the necessary fines that kept him from being sent to prison, but the government garnished his income for the rest of his life. Each month he was allowed to keep a modest amount of money for his living expenses; what remained went to pay his back taxes. No longer able to afford the rent, in 1961, he was forced to leave his much-loved apartment at Amster Yard. He moved into a studio apartment at 166 East Sixty-first Street. Ironically, the design and decoration of this apartment was photographed and published more than any of his other work.

While Baldwin was in the midst of the income tax debacle, he met Edward Lee Cave, a young man from Virginia who was on Albert Hadley's staff. Reeling from the shock of all that had happened to him, Baldwin sought the company of this sympathetic new friend. Cave, a recent graduate of Columbia University, had a refined knowledge of the decorative arts. He and Baldwin frequently dined together, and once a month they planned an excursion outside of the city. Baldwin did not drive and enjoyed being chauffeured by Cave. At a time when Baldwin was most vulnerable, Cave provided a much-needed, vital support. Long after Baldwin moved to Nantucket, he and Cave remained friends. Cave went on to become a leading realtor in New York City.

# Gains and Losses

In early 1971, Baldwin made his assistant, Arthur Smith, a partner in his firm and the name was changed to Baldwin, Martin & Smith, Inc. Two months after Baldwin's seventieth birthday, on July 1, 1973, the company was sold to Arthur Smith and the firm was renamed Arthur E. Smith, Inc. Baldwin had worked in the decorating trade for fifty years and most definitely retired while he was still at the top of his game. For the next four years he continued to live in New York City and spend his summers in Nantucket.

The year before he sold his business, he published *Billy Baldwin Decorates*, which is a collection of how-to articles that he had written for *House & Garden*. The book was an immediate success and had three printings in one year. His second book, *Billy Baldwin Remembers*, was published the year after he retired. Like his book on decorating, it was very well received. Some of his most noted commissions were completed just before he sold his firm to Arthur Smith, which gave the shelter magazines an enormous backlog of stories and photographs yet to be published. Even though he was officially retired and had closed his office, Baldwin's work was news well into the eighties.

During an interview for Andy Warhol's *Interview* magazine at his apartment at East Sixty-first Street shortly after his retirement, Baldwin revealed a fact that his friends had known for years. He said to the interviewer, Brigid Polk [Berlin], "I have no money. I have retired in absolute poverty, I promise you. And you have to believe this, my sweet child, because I am not going to tell you anything that is not true. I live on a small pension and my Social Security. Because I don't care about money, I never once gave a thought to making money. My firm, however, did very well. I suppose I should have behaved myself in New York—I loved books, clothes, the theater—and spent an awful lot of money. But nobody worked harder than I did or loved decorating more."

He continued, "Now, this is everything I have in the world—everything that you see here in this one-room apartment is all I have. I consider that I have luxury because, first of all, that bathroom has a window in it so I get daylight. I don't have to turn on the electric light in the bathroom in the morning. This saves money. My little kitchen has a window and again I have daylight. What more in the world should I want? What I love the most are my books. I don't own a television. I love to read and write letters."

PRECEDING PAGE

*A view of Baldwin's writing table, looking into his apartment, 166 East Sixty-first Street, New York City. The Korean screen behind the Lawson sofa had been with him since 1946 when he decorated his apartment at Amster Yard.* Photo by Horst.

FACING PAGE

*A corner of the living area of Baldwin's apartment at 166 East Sixty-first Street, New York City. The black-and-white paintings above the Louis XV chair are by Al Held.* Photo by Horst.

ABOVE

*Painting of Baldwin's apartment by Jeremiah Goodman.*

This view of Baldwin's apartment on East Sixty-
first Street shows the Saint Thomas-style sofa that
served as his bed. The eighteenth-century English
painting of two dogs above the sofa was one of
Baldwin's prized possessions. He referred to the two
dogs as "Carlos de Beistegui and me," meaning that
the large hound was de Beistegui. When Woodson
Taulbee acquired a house in Old San Juan, Puerto
Rico, Baldwin decorated the house and gave the
painting to Taulbee. *Photo by Horst.*

*A corner of the living area of Baldwin's apartment,*
*166 East Sixty-first Street, New York City. On the*
*cane-wrapped Parsons table is a pair of sculptures*
*by Pericle Fazzini, "The Diving Boys."* Photo by Horst.

He also noted, "I have a great many things scattered around the room, and I have to tell you quite truthfully they have all been given to me by friends or clients. I dread Christmas because I am afraid that I'm going to get another cigarette box or ashtray. I wish my friends would give me a pound of caviar or, better, a check."

When he was questioned about his days in the decorating trade, Baldwin remembered, "I never had anything but the wildest pleasure. Although it can be a hell of a profession. Every woman in America thinks she's a born interior decorator. They all say, 'I want to give you complete freedom, but . . .' My whole life has been one long battle against the 'buts.' Someone might tell you, 'We like everything "but" the curtains.' For me the curtains were the whole point of the room. If the client insisted that I change them, I'd feel that the room had been robbed of anything to do with me.

"The ideal is to have a client with whom you are sympathetic. I always felt obligated to do my best to make my clients happier, but I was firm in my opinions. My work was confined to the struggles, the agonies, and the joys of my clients and what they had: money, children, cats or dogs or both, upkeep, country houses, city houses, apartments, and houses abroad. The important thing was to keep our relationship a pleasure, from beginning to end."

"In many ways, I've been very lucky. I think luck matters an awful lot. Luck and hard work are what it's all about. I have very few regrets—one or two jobs I turned down because I was afraid, and a few that I should not have undertaken I unfortunately accepted. I have very, very few regrets in my personal life. If I had to describe myself to someone, I say I'm a fairly dignified man with enormous enthusiasm.

"I don't think I was ever unreasonable, but I was very strict. Not one bad stitch got by me. I was exacting and people called me a perfectionist. I would have been miserable if someone had pointed to a shabby piece of furniture and said, 'Can you believe that Billy Baldwin made that horrible sofa,' as I often heard about other decorators.

"You have to remember that gossip is the essence, the basis, of conversation in the decorating world. Believe me, you could never tell anybody anything. There are some decorators who survive on gossip. They carry it along with their samples of chintz. In Baltimore, it would be very scandalous if Mrs. So-and-So had a lover, but in New York it was gossip about people's houses. People would love to gossip about Mr. and Mrs. So-and-So having perfectly terrible curtains. They gossip more about houses than women's clothes."

Baldwin's reputation for being a gossip was one of the reasons ladies liked to take him to lunch. One of

his clients remembered, "He was better than a gossip column and knew everything about everybody." His former boss, Ruby Ross Wood, always said, "Billy B is small but his sting is deep."

Susan Marcus, a member of the Dallas family who founded Neiman Marcus, first met Baldwin at a dinner party Mary Wells and Harding Lawrence gave to celebrate the house that he had decorated for them in Dallas. She recalls, "He was absolutely mesmerizing. We sat down and he began to tell me about his work. I was so captivated that we never went into dinner. I cannot begin to tell you how enchanting Billy was and I am not alone in this. Everyone who knew him felt the same way. He was over seventy and yet he had the enthusiasm of a young convert."

Most of his clients knew that when Baldwin retired he had little money. Most of them were aware that the IRS allowed him to keep only a small allowance for his living expenses. One of his clients found out that he was not allowed to rent the small house on Nantucket, Chanticleer Cottage, because the IRS deemed it an unnecessary expense. She decided to pay the rent each summer. When Baldwin was invited to visit someone, his host or hostess always said, "I will arrange your travel and send you a ticket." He had no choice but to accept the generosity of his wealthy friends. Not having the means to return these generous favors, Baldwin repaid his friends with fierce loyalty.

Baldwin's enduring loyalty was keenly evident when he decorated Woodson Taulbee's house in San Juan, Puerto Rico, in 1973.

Baldwin recalled the house was in the old part of San Juan. "When Woody bought the house, there were eight families living there. There was nothing really on the outside, but the glory of the house, the magic, happened when you opened the door of what appeared to be a very small house. You came through the entrance door into a hall."

"The whole house had to be gutted. Some of the beams were rotten—only some could be used—and the ground floor was made of mud. The new floor of the entrance hall was created from old marble that came from another house. The entrance hall led into a large drawing room. New tile floors there went through all of the rooms with no interruption opening onto a new patio that the owner built."

"Woody and I did not try to follow any traditional Puerto Rican ideas for decorating a house. We were very free to introduce all kinds of things. I thought it would be nice to use furniture from India because of the romance associated with India. In fact, furniture from India may well have been brought to the house many years ago. The house had no dining room as such but in the main living area we created a dining area. It was furnished with low chairs that revolved. I gave my most prized possession, a large eighteenth-century English portrait of two hunting hounds, for this room."

Baldwin always said that the dogs, one extremely large and the other very small, were "Carlos Beistegui and me."

The year after the house was finished, Woodson Taulbee died of lung cancer. He was sixty-six. Taulbee was the first of a group of Baldwin's friends who died in the seventies. A heavy smoker since his teenage years, Baldwin realized that he must quit. Although he stopped, the damage was done and he suffered from severe emphysema in his last years.

Lung cancer claimed another of his dearest friends in 1976. Babe Paley died in New York City after a long battle with the disease. That same year, Pauline [Potter] de Rothschild died in Santa Monica, California, and Helen Hull died at her country estate on the Hudson River. Baldwin grieved deeply for these women who had meant so much to him. Three years later, in April 1979, Van Day Truex died. There is no question that Truex had been his most loyal colleague. Seven months after Truex's death, Kitty Miller died. Her death was more than Baldwin could bear, and he knew the time had come to leave New York City. He made up his mind to move permanently to Nantucket. He had lived in Manhattan for four years after his retirement, but Baldwin decided it was time to heed his own maxim, "A man cannot live in this city without working unless he is very rich."

# The Other Island

Baldwin's decision to move to Nantucket was not without problems. While there were many houses and apartments for rent on Nantucket during the summer months, there were few year-round rentals. Certainly Baldwin did not have the money to buy a house. Michael Gardine and Way Bandy, two men he had known for years, came to his rescue. Gardine was a writer and an antiques dealer; Bandy was a high-fashion makeup artist. They owned a house at 22 Hussey Street in the village of Nantucket. Behind their house was a small outbuilding.

Gardine and Bandy paid for the structure to be converted into a two-room house for Baldwin. The first floor was the living room; above was a small bedroom, bath, and tiny closet. In spring 1980, Baldwin moved into the new house. The walls were painted white, the support beams were left in their natural wood, and each room was anchored with a fireplace.

The simple frame house was far different from the retirement home of another American decorator emerita, the late Elsie de Wolfe, or more properly, Lady Mendl. She retired to a large house, Villa Trianon, in Versailles, France. Remembering her definition of taste as "suitability, simplicity, and proportion," Baldwin said, "Nantucket is as right for me as Versailles was for Elsie. I think I'm lucky to be here on Nantucket and not on Sixty-first Street in Manhattan. I'd be near suicidal if the best view I had was looking at Bloomingdale's."

Baldwin said of his new home, "I've eliminated everything except the details. I like the bones of a structure, retaining the vestige of the architecture. The last place I lived was a one-room apartment. This place is tiny but it's not an apartment. It is a very, very small house. I like it better than any place I have lived since growing up in my family's home in Baltimore. What I love and now realize that I had missed is going upstairs to bed in the evening, and coming down each morning to have the day. It's awfully attractive. I think this house is not only suitable, it is luxurious. Every comfort is here, and the two rooms are all that I could possibly take care of.

"I have come to regard comfort as the ultimate luxury. Comfort for me is a room that works for you and your guests. Luxury is having a table handy to put down a drink or a book. It's also knowing that if

PRECEDING PAGE
*The living room of Baldwin's cottage,*
*22 Hussey Street, Nantucket,*
*Massachusetts. Private collection.*

ABOVE AND FACING PAGE

*Chanticleer cottage, which Baldwin rented for many*
*summers, and a view of the cottage's living room.*
*Nantucket, Massachusetts. Private collection.*

someone pulls up a chair for a talk, the whole room doesn't fall apart. It's deep, upholstered furniture. The trouble with a lot of people is that they misinterpret the true meaning of luxury and confuse it with grandeur, or obviously expensive furnishings. Price is almost totally invalid as a measure of quality or value. A very expensive look is not suitable to the way most of us live today, regardless of our incomes.

"When I first moved into this house I had all of the upholstered furniture covered in plain white linen,

and the whole room just looked blah. Then I found this printed cotton chintz, 'La Portugaise,' at Brunschwig & Fils. The strong bold stripes give a wonderful perk. Now the room is alive, and there is a duet going on with the beams and the chintz. I love it.

"Scale is an important factor in decorating small rooms. The most common mistake that people make is thinking that all the furniture should be one scale—and a small scale at that. But, you know, something wonderful happens when you use some over-scaled pieces in a small room—say, a large table or two large chairs. As long as a room isn't over furnished, the big pieces of furniture will make a small space look larger.

"When you're decorating, you must learn to break rules, but not all of them. Take the case of pattern on pattern. Some decorators today think you can willy-nilly mix prints. Not so. This only results in confusion. There always must be some connection if you are using more than one print. It can be the color, curves, or line, but the connection must be there. I also think it is very important to establish a connection when you mix pieces of furniture that have different provenances. They must become good neighbors. It is possible to place a superb modern table next to an antique chair, but if you put a reproduction table next to an antique chair, it will look wrong. There wouldn't be any connection at all.

"I always tried, when starting a job, to use things that the client owned. But I add a word of caution. Don't use anything just because you have it. If something is not right and doesn't work with the rest of the room, get rid of it. I would rather do without than use something just because I have it. When I moved to Nantucket, I had to get rid of many things, like most of my books. I boiled down my possessions to the things that I really love, but if I came home tomorrow and found the house had been burglarized, there's not a thing I would miss. I find that material things mean less and less."

Among the few objects that Baldwin kept for his new house were nineteenth-century French inkwells made of tortoise shells that had been a birthday gift from Kitty Miller; a miniature antique scrimshaw whale that was a gift from Mary Wells Lawrence; a

paper knife shaped like a fish that belonged to Ruby Ross Wood; and a photograph of Pauline de Rothschild.

In one of his last interviews, when Baldwin was asked if he had developed a philosophy about life, he replied, "Let me start by saying think it was possible for an American man not to work. For some Europeans this may be okay." He believed that in this country, anybody that is worthwhile is a worker, and that work is the secret of happiness.

He also felt an intense responsibility to be of service to his fellow man. Now that he no longer worked as a decorator, he was involved in Nantucket with the church, Meals-on-Wheels, and the library. He needed to feel that he was contributing something. Even though he got paid as a decorator, he liked to think that he provided something for his clients that they could not do for themselves. He interpreted the way that they wanted to live to the best of his ability. When someone would ask, "Billy didn't you do the So-and-So's house?" he would say, "Yes, I worked with them, but we did it together." This means that "the house and the experience of living there is theirs, not mine." This had been Baldwin's attitude for many years, maybe from the time he started working. In an earlier article in the *New York Times* from the mid-sixties, he said, "The relationship between the decorator and client must be 'we.' The worst thing any decorator can do is to give a client the feeling that he's walking around in somebody else's house; the rooms must belong to the owner, not to the decorator; and no rooms can have atmosphere unless they are used and lived in."

While he had to have patience when he worked as a decorator, he realized later that he didn't always give people enough of a chance. He was a small man and his behavior was often a little Napoleonic. He always felt that life was good, that you had to give your best and expect the best from other people. He didn't care about dull people. He never wanted to sit around, yawning, trying to be polite to people who meant nothing to him. He didn't have time for that. On Nantucket he had grown more tolerant. He was much less critical, and he demanded far less. He had become accustomed to people being pleasant and

FACING PAGE AND ABOVE
*Two detail views of Baldwin's bedroom at 22 Hussey Street, Nantucket, Massachusetts. The picture on the left shows his reading chair and the picture above is his small writing nook. Both photographs, private collection.*

considerate. In his final years, he felt that some of his New York friends were perfectly lousy. They came up from the city to visit him and he couldn't wait for them to leave. Some of them suddenly seemed awfully tough. They may have been attractive, bright, and witty but they were not very nice.

As much as Baldwin loved Nantucket, when he moved there he was in his late seventies and suffering from advanced emphysema. It was difficult for him to breathe during the severe winters. Each year, soon after Christmas, he left for warmer climes. With the financial assistance of friends, he was able to rent a room in a small hotel in Palm Beach, Florida. He

extended his sojourns down south with visits to Key West, where he stayed with Michael Gardine and Way Bandy, and he frequently visited Bunny Mellon in Antigua.

By the end of 1980, his second year on Nantucket, life had become increasingly difficult for Baldwin. He continued to be upbeat, but his emphysema drained most of his energy. One of his neighbors, Francis Carpenter, remembers how difficult it was for him to leave his house. When she invited him out for lunch or dinner he barely had the strength to get in

and out of her car. One cold winter day she was delivering some provisions to his house and found him in bed shivering under a thin mohair lap robe. When she offered to get him additional blankets, he told her that the mohair cover was all that he had. She left the house immediately and bought him an electric blanket.

Throughout the fall of 1982, it was often impossible for Baldwin to get out of bed. In no way could he consider going to Florida after Christmas. Fortunately, his tiny house was built to withstand the brutal cold and friends on the island took care of his shopping. The two pastimes that he most enjoyed, reading and writing, could be done in bed. The few surviving letters that he wrote during this time make no mention of his failing health and are, as always, optimistic about the future. In a note to longtime friend, Harry Hinson, Baldwin wrote, "I think about New York. We must meet in the spring, which is not too far away."

Soon after Christmas 1982, Baldwin's breathing became increasingly labored and he was taken to the Nantucket Cottage Hospital. With the aid of oxygen and proper nursing care, he made it through the winter. After five months, and still on oxygen, he was allowed to go home. Memorial Day meant the return of his summer friends, and he had hopes that his life would be happier. Sadly this was not the case.

Being with a group of people and carrying on a conversation required more strength than Baldwin could muster. Michael Gardine and Way Bandy took responsibility for his medicine, monitored the number of visitors he had each day, and saw that he ate a proper diet. Without Gardine and Bandy, Baldwin would have had to live in a nursing home. Whether he was dressed casually or even was in his pajamas and robe, he made every effort to look his best when company came. Though critically ill, Baldwin never let down his standards of good grooming.

Gardine and Bandy usually left Nantucket soon after Labor Day, but because of Baldwin's fragile condition they stayed until mid-October. Baldwin felt that if he had the help of a visiting nurse he could stay in his house. This did not work. Soon after Gardine and Bandy left he was again admitted to the hospital. His

condition continued to deteriorate. On the Friday after Thanksgiving, November 25, 1983, William Williar Baldwin, Jr., died. At his request, there was no funeral or memorial service. His ashes were scattered on the beach in Nantucket.

In his will, filed with the Nantucket probate court on January 17, 1984, Baldwin left most of his possessions to Michael Gardine. A few items—small bronze figures, gold cuff links, cigarette boxes, and leather-bound volumes of rare texts—were designated to go to specific people including Bunny

Mellon, Deeda Blair, Diana Vreeland, Nan Kempner, Louise Grunwald, Mary Wells Lawrence, Babs Simpson, Bill Blass, Edward Lee Cave, and Albert Hadley. These people were among the few in Baldwin's inner circle.

In his obituary in the *New York Times*, which ran on November 26, 1983, Diana Vreeland is quoted as saying, "Decorators have been influenced by Billy ever since he came to New York, particularly by his sense of groupings, and of order, and his ability to do much with not too much, to let a little go a long way. He didn't arbitrarily throw out your furniture and used as much of it as possible if it was any good in the first place. And he didn't believe in clutter. His influence was truly vast. During the time he was active, his sense of order, of arrangement, cast a long shadow over the decorating profession."

A week later, in the *New York Times*, Rita Reif wrote an article entitled "Billy Baldwin: Appraising a Master" that included quotes from his friends and clients. Perhaps the person who best captured Baldwin's spirit was Edward Lee Cave. He said, "Mr. Baldwin was the first influential decorator who was totally American in his outlook." Four years later in the *Times*, Carol Vogel echoed Cave's opinion. She wrote, "Billy Baldwin's interiors—those crisp-lined rooms that epitomized elegance and sophistication from the 1950s through the 70s—had such a powerful effect on design that his name became synonymous with American style."

Baldwin would have been pleased. Many years before, in an article from 1965, he was quoted as saying in the *Times*, "We in this country have the greatest taste level in the world. Maybe it's because we are young; we've always been on the way up and have never had to come down. I can't tell you how American I am."

Ten years after Baldwin's death, in yet another article in the *Times*, Mitchell Owens wrote, "'Cotton is my life,' Baldwin often said. He was fond of blue denim, too, as well as swing-arm brass lamps, white paper shades, matchstick blinds, and rooms loaded with books—to use, he counseled his clients; never just for show. Small wonder so much of his work was copied over the years. He understood the delicate balance between real style and the realities of modern life, particularly the vexations of cramped city living. Bringing grace to small, badly planned apartments was a Baldwin trademark."

Baldwin died nearly thirty years ago. In Susan Gray's book, *Designers on Designers*, published in 2003, the noted New York interior designer Tom Britt said of Baldwin, "When I came to New York to study at Parsons, I met Billy. Well, for me it was just like meeting God. I mean no one, no one, had more influence on interior decorating than Billy Baldwin."

*The bedroom of Baldwin's cottage at 22 Hussey Street, Nantucket, Massachusetts. Private collection.*

PART TWO

# The "Decorating Today" Lectures

# INTRODUCTION

In May 1974, Baldwin gave four lectures on interior decorating at the Cooper-Hewitt, National Design Museum, Smithsonian Institution in New York City. Baldwin had closed his decorating firm, Baldwin & Martin, Inc., the previous year. The following press release came from the museum's archives.

"Billy Baldwin, one of the country's leading interior decorators, will give four lectures on 'Decorating Today' at the Cooper-Hewitt National Design Museum on Wednesday evenings during May. The lectures will be given in the Carnegie Mansion, 2 East 91st Street, at 6:00 p.m. on May 8, 15, 22, and 29.

The lecture series will be devoted to giving information that will be helpful when one undertakes the decorating of a room or a house. It will cover all aspects of decorating—the planning stage, basic architectural structure, furniture, the elements of decoration (color, materials, texture, pattern), and the final touches which make a room personal.

'The Beginning of the Project' will be discussed on May 8, 'The Bones of a Room' on May 15, 'The Elements of Decoration' on May 22, and 'The Personal Touch' on May 29. The lectures are by subscription—$15 for the series, $4 per lecture. Tickets may be ordered through the Education Department at the Cooper-Hewitt Museum.

During his distinguished career of 40 years, Mr. Baldwin decorated the homes of many of the most celebrated and wealthy men and women in the world. He came to New York from Baltimore in 1935 to work for Ruby Ross Wood, who originated the famous 'Au Quatrième' at Wanamaker's [department store in New York]*, and later established his own firm Baldwin & Martin, Inc. His *House & Garden* book, *Billy Baldwin Decorates*, has gone through three printings since it was published by Holt, Rinehart and Winston in 1972. A sequel, *Billy Baldwin Remembers*, will be published by Harcourt Brace Jovanovich, Inc. in October 1974."

* The interior decorator Nancy McClelland started Au Quatrième. When she resigned to open her own firm, Ruby Ross Wood, who was working there, succeeded her.

*The guesthouse at Mill Pond Farm, the country estate of Ambassador Francis L. Kellogg, in Bedford, New York. Photo by Horst.*

# The Beginning of the Project

Today I am going to talk about the most practical aspects of the interior decorating profession. What I have to say might seem a little grim because a lot of it will be very practical information. I will talk about the necessity of a budget and speak directly to the question of money. As the lectures go on, they will be more glamorous.

Let's begin with several possible scenarios in your life. One is that you are going to build a house or you have just bought a house. Two other possibilities are an apartment that you have bought or an apartment that you are renting. In any of the possibilities, I assume you like your new place and are pleased with the location. If you require an architect to build or remodel, you should chose a person whose work you have seen. You should interview him and be sure that he is sympathetic with your ideas and your budget. If you are remodeling an old house, be sure that he is sincerely interested in your project. Not all architects want to work on a remodeling job, they much prefer to build new houses. If you want a modern house, choose an architect who likes modern architecture. If you are a traditionalist, choose a person whose taste is the same as yours. I assume that you will select your decorator for the same reasons that you chose an architect. As soon as you've chosen an architect and a decorator, arrange a meeting that includes both of them and you. Each should respect the other's ability.

In addition to admiring the work of your architect and decorator, you should like them personally and let us hope that they like you. You must give them intrinsic trust. Admit that they know more about accomplishing your wishes than you do. They can materialize your taste through experience and knowledge. State at once the amount of money you can spend and don't be ashamed of it. Where you live should be consistent with your way of living. Honesty is the first rule; you and the architect and the decorator must be honest with one another. Do not be ashamed of simple food, simple architecture, simple decoration, or simple gardens. Be proud of honesty, modesty, and unpretentiousness. There must be sympathy, congeniality, and mutual admiration between you, your architect, and your decorator. There is a lot of hard work ahead, and it must be done with joy and smiles, not scowls.

Many architects dislike decorators and with good reason. They do not want to have their design ruined.

PRECEDING PAGE

*Table set for breakfast, the guesthouse at Mill Pond Farm, the country estate of Ambassador Francis L. Kellogg, in Bedford, New York.* Photo by Horst.

RIGHT

*The guesthouse at Mill Pond Farm, the country estate of Ambassador Francis L. Kellogg, in Bedford, New York.* Photo by Horst.

I always put architecture first but I admit that I have had to cope with some horrors. Many architects build from the outside in, instead of from the inside out. What good is beautiful fenestration if it creates unworkable wall spaces? It is difficult for many people to read blueprints and visualize the spaces. Even if you've seen a house your architect has done, be very clear about what you like and don't like. If you've seen a room with the proportions you like, give the dimensions to the architect—all of them, including, heaven knows, the ceiling height.

At that first meeting there are many things that you should check: the swing of the doors, electrical plugs, the type of window treatment (curtains or shutters?), spaces for beds and bedside tables, lighting in general and the lighting of pictures, the dimensions of pieces of furniture that you own and expect to use, and the size of your favorite rugs. If you are building a new house, as soon as possible visit the construction site together. This togetherness establishes that you, the architect, and the decorator are a team. The same holds true if you are remodeling a house or an apartment. Interior decoration is not an end in itself, but the means to a way of life. There must be continuity, a point of view, from the front door straight through to the kitchen.

If your house is in the country, the interior must be as appropriate to the architecture as the exterior design is to the gardens and the landscape. In his introduction to the book *The Finest Rooms*, Russell Lynes wrote about going to a large white-clapboard house on Long Island with a splendid eighteenth-

*The dining room in the residence of Mrs.*
*Munn Kellogg in Palm Beach, Florida.*
*Photo by Horst.*

*The living room in the residence of Mrs.*
*Munn Kellogg in Palm Beach, Florida.*
Photo by Horst.

century doorway. When he entered the house, totally inappropriate to the exterior he encountered an elaborate Spanish Mission interior, complete with rough plaster walls, wrought iron candlesticks, and a fountain spattering into a tiled pool.

Once I went with a charming lady to see a house that she was building. The construction was just getting underway. It was a very wise move for us to make this trip together. Everything about the visit was delightful: the rolling hills of the countryside, a lovely spring day, and the fruit trees in bloom. The house was beautifully placed on the property. The blueprints revealed that it was to be simple and modern, with clean lines and lots of glass.

Since this was our first meeting, the lady and I had not discussed interior decoration. Declaring that she hated anything modern, she went on to tell me that she did not have one stick of furniture—not even a picture. Immediately, and rather proudly, she announced that, regardless of cost, everything in the house was to be signed Louis XV and Louis XVI furniture. She wanted eighteenth-century Sèvres porcelain and tapestries. I could only think, why on earth wasn't she building a little French chateau? Mind you, if she had a good piece of French furniture or a tapestry that she inherited, I would have been pleased to use it with contemporary furniture. I could not see why she was planning an interior that was totally inappropriate for the modern design of the house. On the way back to the city I explained that I could never achieve what she wanted.

In the first meeting with the decorator and the architect, the client should make it very clear how he or she intends to use the house or apartment. How does the client entertain? Should the rooms have a formal look or a more casual appearance? Does the client want a dining room or will most of their eating be done in the kitchen? How much space does the client need? Be sure to consider books, television, card-playing, a grand piano, children, and dogs and

cats. The architect and decorator must know if the house or apartment is to be used all year-round, only in the summer or winter, or just for weekends.

Once a woman from the Midwest made an appointment to see me. On the morning she came to my office, she brought a sheaf of blueprints. As we went over them, I could see that she was planning a beautiful house. Her love and understanding of the proposed project revealed that she had done a lot of the planning. She told me that she had studied my work from photographs in magazines and had seen some rooms that I decorated. She said that she had investigated four architects and gone to see their work. In her conversation she admitted that one very good house she saw was designed by a man whose personality she disliked; wisely, he was eliminated. I knew and liked the architect she had settled on and admired his work. She wanted to know if I liked the plans and [asked if] I would make suggestions for the furnishings without changing the overall concept. When I agreed to do this, she had her team in place. That morning we talked for about three hours. Her enthusiasm was contagious, and we both got more and more excited about the project. Finally, she said that she had been told something about me that really worried her. Rather timidly she said that I had a reputation for being unwilling to work for someone unless I liked them. Then she asked, "Do you like me?"

My response was, "Do you like me?" We both broke into laughter and that morning was the beginning of one of the happiest experiences of my life.

I mentioned before that she had her team. In other words, she had made a very definite decision about her architect and her decorator. The key word

Two views of Baldwin's second New York apartment at 2 Sutton Place South. The sofa and club chair are covered in pale blue leather. The antique white satin curtains are hand painted with figures of dancers, "Les Sylphides," in blue, black, and olive green. *Photos by Samuel H. Gottscho.*

here is "decision." Being able to make a decision is absolutely important for a vital, fresh result. Let "decision" be your best friend. You must discipline yourself to be able to make up your mind and not always be changing what you want. Indecision is the enemy of a good decorating job. It stifles the creative spirit of the architect and decorator. When a client can't make up her mind or is constantly changing her mind, she kills the enthusiasm and interest, both physically and intellectually, of the people who are working with her. Indecision cuts all the arteries; the heart will not beat. A room will be dead before it is born.

One day, quite late in the afternoon, I was asked if I could see a couple passing through New York on their way from Mexico to their home in Madrid. When they came in, the charming lady had an enormous briefcase jammed with photographs taken from magazines of rooms that she liked. Quite a few of them were pictures of rooms that I had done. This was encouraging. She also had pictures of rooms that she disliked. In her modest way, she said, "You know, sometimes it is easier to say what you dislike than what you like." That is absolutely true. Anyway, I said I would love to help them. They had an apartment in Madrid located two blocks from the Ritz and one block from the Prado. The apartment had a country-house atmosphere, with lovely balconies looking down upon the municipal botanical gardens.

We discussed, more or less, the look that they had in mind and what they wanted in the way of color. One of the first things they told me about was their interest in contemporary paintings and fine antiques. I was expected to shop for antiques in New York, Paris, and London. They wanted the apartment to be very personal and to have none of the heaviness of Spanish antiques. Everything was to be French, Italian, or English. Quite remarkably, they agreed that every single thing for the apartment would be made in New York City. By this I mean all of the curtains, the carpets, and the upholstered furniture.

I was given a very excellent floor plan from their Madrid architect. Of course, it was in meters but that wasn't all bad. Four weeks later I went to Madrid with plans for the arrangement of furniture fabric samples. I will quickly say I never think it is a good idea to flood people's minds with too many choices. I presented them with two schemes. In four days we made every decision. There was no vacillation, no indecision whatsoever. When I was ready to return to New York, I was even able to leave paint chips with the painters.

I think it was about six weeks later that I went back to approve the paint samples. I was instantly struck by the attitude of the painters and other workmen. Everybody was always smiling. They all ate a lot of lunch and took a nice long siesta in the afternoon. Once they were back on the job, there seemed to be no quitting time. If a man was in the middle of painting a railing, he would finish it all instead of letting it wait until the next morning. I'm afraid we have too little of this attitude in New York City. Anytime we were working on a color and the hour got later and later, the painters would never think of stopping until it was right. In other words, there was the dignity of man, which means pride and cheerfulness. This is tragically lacking in the United States.

A few weeks after I returned to New York City, I called the couple on the telephone to see how things were going. With great enthusiasm they said, "The dining room is going to be beautiful."

I responded, "What do you mean the dining room is 'going to be beautiful'? Isn't it finished?"

"Oh, no." she said. "The painter comes every Saturday and paints a little and leaves."

I would come to understand that while the workmanship was beautiful, nothing was going to hurry anybody. If the truth be known, there was no reason to hurry. It was going to be beautifully done and my clients were living comfortably at the Ritz with their three remarkable children. I would find that all of the children had extraordinarily different personalities and each one cared a great deal about his or her little room. I loved the final results of the house.

I am now going to talk about what I call "terms." For many years I had a business firm, Baldwin & Martin, Inc., but I am no longer involved. The first thing that I did when I accepted a job was to charge an up-front design fee. This fee was based on the size of the job: a single room, a small apartment, a large apartment, a duplex, a house. Each of these took a differ-

*The living room of Baldwin's second New York apartment at 2 Sutton Place South in New York City. The painted white breakfront is fitted with shirred olive green fabric. Photo by Samuel H. Gottscho.*

ent amount of time and commitment. This fee covered all of my travel expenses, such as taxis and car services, but it did not cover train or airplane travel. I never charged an hourly fee. Once the contract was signed, this design fee was nonrefundable and none of the purchase commissions were charged against it. Purchase commissions were additional.

The principle under which we operated was to buy at wholesale and sell to the client at retail. Nothing was hidden from the client. Anyone can see the price on the tag of a fabric sample and they know that professionals get one-third off of this price. Our profit

makes it possible for us to pay the rent, meet the office expenses, pay our business taxes, and have a personal income. The most important thing for me was always getting an estimate. I would not do even a lampshade for a client without an estimate. Whatever the scope of a job, be it thirty dollars, three hundred dollars, or thirty thousand dollars, there was always an estimate. There were two copies of every estimate: one for the client and one for my office records. I would sign both copies and send them to the client. The client kept one copy, signed the other copy, and returned it with a deposit check in the amount of fifty

Baldwin used a red, brown, and cream overscaled English chintz that was strong enough to meet the English needlepoint rug that he put in the living room of this Vermont house. The painting on the left is by Mary Cassatt; the one over the mantel is by Edouard Manet. *Photo by Louis H. Frohman.*

*Baldwin used an East India Company print on the bed and for the curtains in the man's guest room in Greenwich, Connecticut. The Edwardian-style tufted chair is covered in green raw silk. Photo by Louis H. Frohman.*

percent of the total cost. Now, that is not in any way a reflection on the client's credit. It simply makes it possible for a firm to do business. I never thought that I was supposed to be the client's banker. Every good client understands this. People don't want to have to pay a huge amount of money when a job is completed. The fifty-percent deposit that I was paid covered the deposits that were required on any special orders. I had to pay this so that I could discount my bills. Clients were expected to pay in full when the job was satisfactorily completed. I'll just tell you one more thing. Whenever I had a job out of New York City, I always charged for travel time and expenses. My method of doing business was very, very simple.

I consider decorating a business and I conducted the affairs of my firm from a businessman's point of view. I have absolutely no time for these pretty little society girls, recently divorced women or, poor souls, the little widows who think, "What fun it would be to be a decorator." They know nothing about business and, in most cases, nothing about decorating.

In the early part of the century, Elsie de Wolfe, who became Lady Mendl, was given the marvelous job of decorating the second floor of what is now the Frick Museum. This is where Mr. Frick and his family lived. She was paid a ten percent commission on everything, and Mr. Frick spent many many millions. This one job established Elsie de Wolfe forever. What she did in those early days and her ideas, even from the very beginning, influenced everything about decorating today. She was perfectly crazy about getting that ten percent on everything. She really never got over it. In Palm Beach, she even called the local liquor store and the butcher and said, "Of course, I get ten percent of all that the So-and-Sos spend because I recommend them to you." She would go out for dinner and insist on getting ten percent off the bill for the meal. I call it having your beef and eating it, too.

We will now touch on what I consider the ultimate combination. We had been speaking before of a trio—that is, the client, the architect, and the decorator. Now, I will talk about the luxury of a quartet—that is, husband and wife, architect, and decorator. When you have the full quartet, the job is about "we." Everyone can say, "We did this together. The well-functioning quartet allows us to agree and disagree together. When the husband and wife quarrel with each other and disagree about what is happening on a project, they can kill the job. Instead of working on the couple's dreams, the architect and decorator face a nightmare. Having said this, I will now say that when a couple agrees on what they want, the most complete, harmonious results occur. Today there are men who are genuinely interested in architecture and the house where they will live. It is, in a way, a kind of Men's Lib. These men are decisive, and they trust you like they would a fellow businessman. They speak to you in a man-to-man manner. I'll be perfectly honest and say that some men are interested in their house because it is an investment or because their house is a status symbol. By the way, I detest that phrase, "status symbol."

I know several instances where the man of the house is "the collector" and buys all of the art. In some cases, it is because he really loves paintings. I don't know if this is related, but when I came to New York City in 1935, all of the leading decorators were women. Today, with some brilliant exceptions, most of the leading decorators are men. It is also interesting to note that as yet we have very few leading architects who are women. One last word on couples, husbands and wives, and decorating commissions: There are times when the husband has absolutely no interest in the decorating of his house. He completely absents himself from the project and cheerfully pays the bills. This is often the hoped-for ideal.

Speaking again of the great lady decorators, I would like to quote one of them, Miss Anne Urquhart, of the decorating firm Smyth, Urquhart and Marckwald. In the book *The Finest Rooms*, Miss Urquhart describes the perfect decorator. She said, "First: The talent, taste, and background of knowledge and tradition needed to design beautiful rooms of many different kinds, all suitable frameworks for present-day living. Second: A psychological insight good enough to understand the wishes of an inarticulate client who can't describe the atmosphere she wants, and to recognize the right time to encourage some experimental idea even when faced with the 'my husband wouldn't like it' defense. Third: The brain of an IBM computer to be able to answer quickly that first question, 'What will it cost to furnish this apartment?', to stay within a budget, and to keep one's own business solvent while holding the creative side of the work always in first place. Fourth: The drive and capacity needed to pull together all the separate elements of the work and to get the job done on time." How many of these qualifications can your decorator provide?

I know that what I have talked about thus far can be a little boring, but it is absolutely necessary to honestly consider these issues in order to have happy results for you and your decorator. I have tried to tell you some basic things. Things that will help you if you are a client or want to be a decorator. Things that will help you get through this experience in the most pleasant way.

*Baldwin used a black-and-white tartan wall-to-wall carpet in this guest room in Greenwich, Connecticut. The wallpaper is a Woodson Taulbee paper. The green shamrock design in the paper is reflected in the window treatment and the other fabrics in the room.*
Photo by Louis H. Frohman.

# The Bones of a Room

The bones of a room are like the bones of a body, the skeleton. The bones relate to architecture, structure, and things that are permanent. Decoration is the flesh and superficial by comparison. We bake the cake first—architecture. Then and only then comes the icing—decoration. First there are the walls of the room. They surround you. You always see them and are always aware of them. They divide you from the great out-of-doors. They create the great indoors. Let's begin by thinking about wall covering and color.

If you say to your decorator, "I dream of a clear sky blue room," nine times out of ten, the sky blue walls are what you are seeing in your mind's eye. There are many ways to accomplish this clear, fresh blue. With much patience, the perfect color can be mixed, but you will never know if you have achieved what you want until the paint is completely dry. Another way to get the desired color is to glaze white over blue. I want to give you a word of caution. Glazing is antiquing or striating. This means streaking one color over the base color. The application is then rubbed off with cheesecloth or a stiff brush until the thickness or thinness that you are looking for is achieved. This process is not to be confused with a gloss finish or shine that looks like lacquer.

There are also many lovely blues in vinyl. Some of them are very shiny, like patent leather; some have a matte finish like linen. Nothing is more practical than vinyl, and you can paint right over it when your blue bubble has burst and you want another color. Today, all wallpaper can be treated so that it can be carefully washed, not scrubbed, and it is not as tough as vinyl.

Finally, the most luxurious wall covering is fabric. This is achieved by stretching the fabric over the walls. First, wood strips must be put along all the edges, the baseboard, and at the bottom of the crown molding. Then cotton flannel is applied within the borders created by the wooden strips. Beginning at the outer edge of the wooden strips, the fabric is stretched over the cotton flannel. The finishing technique is to glue braid over all of the edges to cover the tacks. All of this is very expensive.

A further practical additional expense is to apply plastic on the plaster walls before the wooden strips and cotton flannel are applied. This is particularly advisable on outside walls in the city. Dust has a way of seeping through mortar. Fabric on the walls is also a great acoustical luxury. Any fabric can be used—even silk or velvet, if that suits your way of life. You may prefer something less formal like cotton or linen. Cotton fabric can also be laminated and hung like wall-

paper. Even with the cost of laminating, this is much cheaper than covering the walls with fabric.

Walls can also be covered in leather. This is both beautiful and lasting. It is especially attractive when leather is applied in squares in a library. There are also vinyls that look like leather, and they are also attractive.

Then there is the wood-paneled room. The boiseries of the seventeenth and eighteenth centuries were painted or stained with wax to give the color of honey. I do not approve of reproduction period paneled rooms. In a modern room, pale unfinished wood treated very simply can add an element of depth and warmth to a chilly, clinical wall. This may be because the wood itself was once a living tree.

Walls can be covered inexpensively by hanging a rod along the bottom of the crown molding and shirring fabric to hang to the floor. It is not at all necessary to line the fabric. Curtains are made by using bands of the fabric to tie back the wall hangings at the window openings. The curtains, however, must be lined so that when daylight comes through, the fabric matches the color of the wall hangings. I've done this with inexpensive cotton prints, especially fabrics printed in small Near Eastern patterns. If the fabric is fairly thick, the walls do not have to be painted—only the woodwork and the ceiling. Recently I painted a

bedroom yellow and hung very sheer embroidered muslin over the walls. The woodwork was painted white. The fabric can be washed and preshrunk before it is hung so that it can easily be laundered.

If I were to build a house today, without question it would be contemporary. But if I fell in love with an old house, I would enjoy the excitement of making it belong to me. In a modern house I would want more glass than walls. Having worked with people's contemporary houses, I find that sooner or later, mostly sooner, some kind of covering, be it curtains, blinds or shutters, becomes necessary. A room needs protection from glare, unpleasant weather, and the sinister black night. Don't forget that glass becomes a mirror at night, and constantly seeing reflections may make you nervous and uncomfortable.

Having said this, I now say there is nothing more glamorous than a mirrored wall. Walls covered in mirror can be mysterious and also give wonderful reflections of light. If you are remodeling, remember that putting mirror on the walls is much less expensive than knocking down the walls. If you have a pretty view out of a window, try putting mirrors on the wall exactly opposite the window. You get two windows for the same rent. I will give you a warning. In dining rooms and sitting rooms, do not place the mirrored wall so that people sit looking at themselves. You will find that people are fascinated to watch themselves talking and eating, and they end up smiling and grimacing at their own images. It is very hard to resist the fascination of our own image. Finally, I have used mirrors more often in town than in the country.

If you consider wallpaper for your walls, the designs are limitless. They come in every color and every period. Today most papers can be vinyl coated. Thank heaven we are freed from the belief that paintings can only be hung on plain walls. Striped backgrounds do wonders for groups of small pictures and drawings. In the American Embassy in London, a Van Gogh and a Gauguin hang in a vast drawing room that has a fantastic Chinese paper on the walls. The paintings never looked more brilliant and the paper had never been more complemented. After all, Bonnard painted his glorious pictures in a studio where the walls were hung in toile de Jouy. Beside the windows there must be necessary openings in walls for entering and leaving rooms. How do you feel about these openings? Do you want to be able to close them, to close yourself in? We are now talking about doors. I agree with the English and European idea of being able to close off a room with doors. Certainly this gives more privacy and a certain coziness. If doors are open, you are conscious of the movement in the adjoining room. Conversation and concentration may be interrupted by restless movement in the other room. If there are guests in the house, closed doors give them, and you, the freedom to come and go without feeling obliged to speak to each other every time someone passes an open doorway.

Libraries most certainly should have doors for peace and quiet. Children should be taught to knock before entering a room and to close doors behind them after entering or leaving. It is extremely attractive to have dining room doors closed before a meal and open them to see the surprise of a pretty table. After the meal is over and the table has been cleared, and the room is in order, the doors may be left open. If there are no servants to immediately clear the dining room, after the meal everyone can retire to the living room and the doors can be closed.

A New York apartment that I have been in many times has a square entrance hall with four doors: one leading to the living room, one to the dining room, another to the library, and, finally, one that leads to the bedroom corridor. The doors are always kept closed and opened as each room is to be used. The door moldings are black, and the walls and doors are painted high-gloss white. The floor of the hall is covered in a wall-to-wall carpet that has a small black-on-white pattern. There is no room for pictures, only one console table with a mirror above and two benches. There are spotlights over each door. This entrance hall has great style and serves as a tempting overture to the rest of the apartment.

If you have a wide opening I recommend double doors instead of one large, awkward door. With double doors, it is a good idea to keep the one on the left permanently closed. The closed door creates a screen of sorts, and you do not have the illusion of falling through a big opening into a room. Naturally the

*S. I. Newhouse, Jr.'s bedroom in his
townhouse in New York City. The walls and
ceiling were covered in dark brown velvet.
On the left is a painting by Mark Rothko, a*
*Morris Louis painting faces the bed. The
small lithograph is by Barnett Newman and
the sculpture on the extreme right is by Paul
Feeley.* Photo by William Grigsby.

open door should be wide enough for a person to
walk through comfortably.

Doors can be very decorative or they can be made to
disappear. Doors that disappear are called flush doors,
and the surface is treated like the wall. There is no trim
on a flush door, but the baseboard of the room continues across the bottom of the door. Louvered doors,
especially good in tropical houses, allow air and filtered
light to move from room to room. With great advantage, lacquered, wallpapered, or fabric-covered screens
may be applied to doors. Don't forget the sparkle and
reflective quality of mirrored doors. You can change the
whole dimension of a narrow passageway by using mirrored doors. Padded leather or padded vinyl doors are
ideal for a library. Doors upholstered in felt are often
used to soften the sounds in dining rooms. In garden
rooms it is interesting and quite attractive to marbleize

the doors or paint them to look like bamboo. All of my
suggestions depend on the location of the door. If you
build a house, remember that any door or pair of doors
can be made to disappear, slide into the walls.

These are called pocket doors, and when the walls
are wide enough there can be moldings on both
sides. If you use pocket doors, be sure that they are
heavy enough to slide easily and quietly. When a slid-
ing door is too light and flimsy, you have to fight to
get it open or closed.

There is an endless selection of door fixtures at all
prices—knobs, push plates, escutcheons, and hinges.
These are the details that can turn the most banal
apartment door into a thing of beauty—to behold
and to handle.

At the bottom of every room is the floor. It is the
base on which everything rests and from which every-

FACING PAGE

*A country house decorated in the Georgian style. Baldwin used red-and-green plaid wool for the chairs and curtains and a pale green on the sofas. Private collection.*

thing rises. The selection of floor depends very definitely on two things: the rooms we sit in and the rooms we walk in. Rooms that we live in should be quiet spaces. The floors should lie down. They should not jump up and say hello. When you are sitting in a room, the floors should not call attention to your feet. When this happens you feel that you are upside down. If you choose a brilliant-colored carpet, you must use other brilliant color in the room. If you don't, the carpet will stand out above everything else. If you are using a rug instead of wall-to-wall carpet, it should be quite large, surrounded by a border of floor that is eighteen to twenty-four inches. This allows you to arrange all of the furniture on the carpet or all off. This also controls the clatter of high heels. By no means does this demand a plain, dull, beige carpet. In the twenties there was an epidemic of taupe. It was very depressing. People felt that if they had pattern drapery fabric and pattern upholstered furniture, they must have a plain, dead floor. Essentially, they wiped out the base of the room. David Hicks of London had a great influence in liberating the public from this fallacy. His revival of small patterns on rugs and carpets grew into bold geometric designs. First of all, pattern carpet and rugs are far more practical. They show dirt much less and wear much less quickly. Don't let anyone persuade you that a plain, dull carpet is more practical. They show every footprint and become dingy. I'm perfectly agreeable to wall-to-wall carpeting. In fact, I prefer it in city bedrooms. Wall-to-wall carpeting can be a "smoother-outer" in an ill-proportioned room with juts and jags. If you have an ugly floor, cover it up. Wall-to-wall carpet will also soften the sound in a room.

Of course there is nothing more beautiful than eighteenth-century parquet floors. But in all honesty, wooden floors in the country do not have to be parquet. If a country house has old floors, they should be left unfinished and be highly waxed. If you have a country house with new floors, why not paint them with coat upon coat of deck paint or white enamel. And remember, if you use small rugs, the fewer the better. Always place them so that your feet are on them when you are seated.

Don't hesitate to use small rugs right on top of a small-pattern wall-to-wall carpet. If you do this, the smaller rug should have a larger, bolder pattern and be stronger in color. I am talking about the kind of design that is seen in floral bouquets on needlepoint rugs. Another choice, and a good one, is a small Bessarabian rug. Finally, you could even consider Moroccan or contemporary rugs in bold black, white, and brown designs. If the floor is bare, dark, and shiny, a pale, thin, small-pattern Oriental, faded and ancient, is a joy forever. Whatever you choose for small accent rugs, be sure that your little jewels are firmly anchored. They can be sewn onto wall-to-wall carpet or a large area rug. Secure them with a thin rubber under mat on bare floor. Nothing is more irritating or dangerous than a slippery small rug.

Never buy an old rug, large or small, that is already falling to pieces. It is a hazard for walking and the annual maintenance is prohibitive. Also, be sure to put backing on any parts of an old rug that is fraying. When making your rug selection, don't overlook the possibility of raffia or sisal rugs. Both of these materials can be used for wall-to-wall carpet. On a beige terrazzo staircase, I used a sisal runner that was secured by brass rods at the base of each riser. I think all staircases should have runners. Most important, they are a safety factor and keep you from breaking your neck. Runners also absorb the noise of going up and down stairs, particularly the bang of high heels and the constant patter of little feet.

In the country or by the sea, the best-looking floors are the most practical and, vice versa, the most practical floors are the best-looking. Clay tile, slate, stone, brick, or marble are all great. I even use these hard surfaces in bedrooms. If you do use a hard floor in a bedroom, I recommend putting a small rug by the

bed. No one wants to step out of bed onto a cold floor. I am often asked about using vinyl on floors. It is certainly less expensive than the materials I spoke about and also a lot easier to maintain. In an old mill house that was used as a guesthouse, I used vinyl squares that looked like cordovan leather. In a New York penthouse, I installed large squares of white vinyl. High above the city, the white vinyl made the room seem to float in the sky. Vinyl is especially good in children's rooms. Not only is it durable but it comes in fresh, clean colors.

Painted floors must be done by an expert who has the special techniques that are required. Specialists in painting floors will also give you a finish that will last—something durable. Any wooden floor can be scored in any design and painted any color. They can be brilliant colors or subtle. They can be made to look like anything that you want: malachite, lapis lazuli, or the coolest marble. In an entrance hall or corridor, the painted finish can be on the walls and the floor—the whole room. In a garden room, the floors may well be painted to look like the mosaic tiles of Pompeii. If you ever do this, consider slip-covering all of the furniture in white sailcloth. Let nature do the rest.

It is very fashionable to stain floors very dark. If you like this, do not get the floors so dark that it is impossible to see the wood grain. When this happens, the floors become dense and lifeless. You may want to think of bleached floors or even white floors that have been lightly glazed.

The year after I began working for Ruby Ross Wood, 1935, we decorated a beautiful new house in Palm Beach. The floor of the big living room was to be marble squares that were taken from an old house in Cuba. The marble had mellowed with age and was the color of parchment. When the marble arrived in Florida, there were not enough of the squares to fill the room. Mrs. Wood, the architect, and the owners had agreed that this was the only floor, nothing else would do. After a sleepless night, the dawn broke and I woke up with the idea of putting a two-foot border of bleached oak around the marble floor. The result was more beautiful than the original design. The angel of God had landed on our shoulder.

Having talked at length about floors, I want to now look up and focus on the ceiling. Just for fun, raise your eyes and look at the ceiling in this room. It is the greatest compliment to the decorator that you had not noticed the ceiling until now. It is not about to fall on your head or be carried away to the heavens by a cyclone. If you lose the top of a box, you have no choice but to throw the box away. If your hatband is too tight, you get rid of the hat. A ceiling is another matter. You cannot avoid the ceiling of a room. The correct treatment of a ceiling is one of the most important considerations in any decorating job.

In most of the new postwar buildings, the ceilings are low. In these buildings, it is fatal to have a white ceiling unless the walls are also white. If you live in an apartment with low ceilings and want colored walls, have your painter put a drop of the wall color in the white paint for the ceiling. Keep adding, drop by drop, until the right color is achieved. Almost without exception, the ceiling must be painted with a flat paint. Even when the walls, woodwork, and crown molding have a glossy finish or they are glazed. By and large, painters are a race apart. Do not let them slyly confuse you by talking to you about eggshell enamel. This refers to the texture and shine of an eggshell and has nothing to do with color. Actually an eggshell finish is between a high gloss and a flat finish. It is often called a satin finish.

The successful treatment of a ceiling is often achieved by considering the use of the room. Consider the question: Is the room going to be used more in the daytime or in the evening? A room in the city that is used only at night, even if it has only one exposure, can be dazzlingly beautiful with dark walls and a dark ceiling. Unfortunately, the room becomes a tunnel during the day. Everything disappears and the single opening becomes like the bright headlights of an approaching car. I cannot imagine treating a room in a country house like this.

In tropical houses, walls are almost always white, as they should be. The ceilings should be painted soft, cool colors—pale blues and pale greens. Doing this cuts the cruel glare of the unrelenting sun that tends to make people nervous and irritable. In Latin countries we often see elaborate ceilings—some

*The library/dining room of Mrs. Munn Kellogg in New York City. Photo by Horst.*

are arched, others sculpted and painted—supported by white walls. These ceilings are usually very high, creating tall rooms [that] are most comfortable. In England, in the seventeenth, eighteenth, and nineteenth centuries, the rooms had elaborate and colorful ceilings. They were often painted stucco or plaster. The carpets were often woven with the same design that was in the ceiling. During the same period, the French tended to have less elaborate ceilings.

Ceiling beams can be the bane of one's existence. They can certainly be a challenge to the dec-

orator. The same annoying beams can be made into an asset by staining or painting them. Such treatment must be coherent with the style and atmosphere of the entire room. Sometimes it is wiser to make a feature of beams than to apologize for them. I know a woman who has a big, ugly mouth. It is impossible to reduce the size of her lips, so she has the intelligence to paint them even bigger with the brightest possible red lipstick. It gives her whole personality an added pizzazz. Be brave, try it in your rooms.

# The Elements of Decoration

The first step in decorating and furnishing a room or a house is having an up-to-date floor plan. If a house is being built or has just been built, floor plans should be available. If this is the case, be sure that all of the changes that were made from the first plans to final plans have been added to your drawings. This is most important in the placing of wall sockets, lighting fixtures, telephones, and televisions.

If you are working with an old house or apartment and plans need to be drawn, ask the architect to draw them on a one-half-inch scale. This scale makes it easier and clearer to see the space and to make the necessary considerations for placing the furniture you have and the things that you will need to buy. Clearly seeing and understanding the space allows you to make a list of what you have and what you do not have. The floor plan gives the client, the architect, and the decorator a clear vision. It helps establish the character of the room.

When a house or an apartment is being decorated from scratch and everything is going to be new, we are presented with advantages and disadvantages. I am always happier if there is something that you love

and want to have around you—things that you want to keep. I call this your personal stuff.

Most rooms today are multipurpose rooms. I think that we have said good-bye to the formal parlor. When I am decorating a large house, I do use the term "drawing room" to indicate that it is the most formal and maybe least used room in the house or apartment. I think a room should be comfortable with four people and as many as twenty.

In many cases today, the dining room is gone—a relic of the past. I love houses and apartments where you can eat anywhere. This versatility depends on the number of people, the type of meal, the time of day, and the time of year. When a decorator is planning a room that will have multiple purposes, it is necessary to know how the client expects to use the space. This will determine the choice of materials and colors. Two other very important considerations in planning any space are children and pets.

Decorating would be much easier if all the rooms were perfectly proportioned, but this would also make the decorator's job far less interesting. There is a lot of fun turning a sow's ear into a silk purse. Of course, I prefer a cotton purse. When I am faced with

*The dining room in the Arizona ranch house of Mr. and Mrs. Harding Lawrence. The large painting is by the Greek-American artist Theodoros Stamos.* Photo by Horst.

ABOVE AND RIGHT

*The entrance hall and living room
of the Arizona ranch house of
Mr. and Mrs. Harding Lawrence.
Photos by Horst.*

a room that has windows in the wrong places, odd protuberances, and doors breaking up most of the usable wall space, I say to myself, this ugly situation does not exist. I refuse to linger on the distractions and begin dreaming of the attractive space we will make in spite of everything. It is important to ever keep in mind that we should not make impossible demands of any space.

In drawing up the floor plans, think about furniture placement: It is necessary to work with accurate scale measurements. This has nothing to do with color or fabrics. We do not even think about these things until the plan is crystallized. This is hard for a client to understand. They immediately want to talk about the icing on the cake. This will come, but first the cake. A woman once said to me in the very first steps of preparing the plans, "What about the pillows, and the colors and the fabrics?" I told her that I

*The master bedroom suite
of the Arizona ranch house of
Mr. and Mrs. Harding Lawrence.
Photo by Horst.*

thought we should stop for the day, that she seemed tired. She had forgotten the first thing I told her. The cake comes first, then the icing. When the plan is done, everyone will be quite pleased, I promise you.

It is important to remember that we do not want to spend the entire budget on architectural and structural changes and details. There must be money for the furnishings. The first rule in choosing furniture is suitability and second, durability. This applies to a Louis XV armoire or a contemporary cocktail table. Both must do the job that is intended and they must work efficiently and beautifully. We must always keep in the back of our minds that we may want things that don't exist in the market. This means that we must design or create these things and have them made. If we insist on a special antique, we must wait until we find just the right thing. When we do, we will fall in love with it, and it's worth the wait and the price.

One of the biggest mistakes people make in selecting furniture is skimping on upholstered furniture. The common attitude is that the structure under the fabric doesn't matter. This is a terrible mistake. First of all, I do not think any room that has anything to do with the way we live today can be without upholstered furniture. To me, upholstered furniture is the extended hand of the host or hostess: it is an invitation to sit down, it is the symbol of hospitality. It is hospitality. Of course, in any room there must be chairs with exposed legs and table legs, but if all you see is legs, the signal is "stand up."

I urge you, please invest in the best available custom-made upholstered sofas and chairs. Each piece should be upholstered to the floor, and if you have them slipcovered, they should have a flat skirt to the floor. I don't like kick pleats on upholstered furniture. They give the illusion the sofa or chair is

RIGHT

*The dining room in the apartment of Mr. and Mrs. Harding Lawrence in New York City.* Photo by Horst.

FACING PAGE

*The living room in the apartment of Mr. and Mrs. Harding Lawrence in New York City. The large painting is by Richard Pousette-Dart.* Photo by Horst.

flying away. Upholstered furniture should appear grounded, that it is staying put. Furniture with legs wants to walk around.

When the time comes to select upholstered furniture, I think the client, or clients, if it happens to be a couple, should go to the upholsterer with the decorator. You should sit in the chairs and sofas that you are buying. You should feel like you are wearing the piece of furniture. It is like buying a dress or a suit. You must feel happy, comfortable, and chic or you will be miserable and uneasy.

If you are getting a two-person love seat, ask the question, "Is it wide enough?" A love seat should never be less than four and a half feet between the arms. If the seat is not long enough, you will be forced to sit up as straight as a ramrod with your legs forward. Keep in mind when you are counting how many people can sit in a room, a sofa that is six feet six inches long, or longer, is really only comfortable

for two people. Heaven help the poor soul who has to sit in the middle.

The filling for sofa cushions does not need to be all down. For many people, having all-down cushions is too soft, like having a bed that is too soft. You will get much better support if your cushions have a core of foam rubber between two layers of down. What I am talking about is a foam-rubber sandwich of sorts. This will also keep your sofa looking neat without constantly puffing the cushions. Believe it or not, I have actually seen a hostess start puffing up the cushions the minute her guests get up to leave. How rude can you be! I am not going to mention her name, but believe me what I am telling you is true.

I always recommend attached cushions for the back of a sofa. This is doubly important if you plan to have accent pillows for added luxury and decorative punctuation. Keep always in mind that these added pillows are just that "punctuation" and never the

*The living room in the apartment of Mr. and Mrs. Harding Lawrence in New York City. Photo by Horst.*

essence of grammar. This, "the essence of grammar," is your well-constructed, well-made, beautifully finished sofa.

In the thirties, Ruby Ross Wood developed a completely new chair. Taking the Lawson sofa for her inspiration, she came up with an armless Lawson chair. It is wide enough to seat two people when extra seating is needed. The greatest advantage comes when one is seated alone in the chair. Free from the arms that confine us in chairs, in Mrs. Wood's chair, the single person can freely turn—saddle, if you will—to the left or right for conversation. While it is wonderful for socializing, it is not the best for reading. Without arms there is no book support. From Mrs. Wood's large version, Pauline de Rothschild and I came up with the idea of a much smaller one. I use these smaller ones by the dozen in bedrooms, draw-

ing rooms, libraries—even on roof-covered terraces. I use them in very sophisticated houses in the city and in less formal houses in the country. Children love them because they can easily move them about. The chairs weigh about as much as a stool. Big men with long legs love them; small women with short legs love them. They are my all-time favorite chair.

Please understand that I am not suggesting these small armless chairs as a substitute for a lounge chair. They are not appropriate for an evening of reading or for putting your head back for a short nap. These chairs are best for conversation, for watching television, or in a large bathroom next to the bathtub. When used near the bath, I suggest slipcovering them in Turkish toweling. You will not find a better chair for putting on your shoes. It doesn't matter if you upholster them in needlepoint, suede, leather, vel-

*Mr. Harding Lawrence's dressing room in
his apartment in New York City. The facing
page shows the curtains open to reveal the
hanging space and shelves. Photos by Horst.*

veteen, raw silk, chintz, or Egyptian cotton. They can
be finished in self-welting, elaborate trim; simple nail-
head trim; flat skirt; or long brocade fringe. These little chairs are snobs, but they are at home anywhere.

Over and over, I keep talking about slipcovers. I
cannot think of upholstered furniture and not think
about slipcovers. I advise all of my clients to have their
furniture upholstered in a neutral-color cotton twill
or linen. It is slightly more expensive than muslin.
Then I believe the furniture should be slipcovered.
The slipcovers can be any material, even soft leather.
They may have self-welting or no welts at all. They can

be made to fit very tightly so they look just like upholstery. I prefer a loose-fitting slipcover, like the ones
that are used in England and in France. It takes a sympathetic artist to get the look you want, but hire the
best person available. It is more expensive to do what
I am suggesting because you pay twice for the labor—
once for the upholstery, again for the slipcover. It also
takes more material.

Finally, I also suggest that you have two sets of slipcovers: one for the summer and another for the rest
of the year. Each set is completely removable and can
be sent out to the cleaners. When you change them

each season, it is like greeting an old friend. This also gives you two distinctly different settings in the same room. It is like redecorating with the seasons.

We now come to the subject of tables. This is where we can achieve infinite variety by not having any two tables in the same room the same height. The exception is when two tables hold a pair of lamps, but even then the tables do not have to be a pair. The number-one rule of thumb in tables is that they should be a generous size. Even small pull-up tables should be large enough for an ashtray and a drink. Large tables by the bed are an absolute necessity. This is especially

true in a guest room. In addition to the things that you put on the bedside table for your guests, like an alarm clock, a notepad, and a pencil; a water container and glass on a tray; a box of tissues; several new magazines and the daily newspaper, you will need to leave room for their personal things. It is a good idea for bedside tables—all of them—to have a drawer and a shelf below. You can have extra space on a bedside table if you have wall-mounted lamps on either side of the bed. This is also better for reading.

Do not have coffee tables that are too low. Martha Graham may be a genius, but it is not becoming for a

LEFT AND
FACING PAGE

*The family room in the
apartment of Mr. and
Mrs. Harding Lawrence
in New York City, is seen
here and on the following
page. The painting over
the black Chesterfield
sofa is by Kenzo Okada.
The painting above
the mantel is by
Helen Frankenthaler.*
*Photos by Horst.*

woman to have to squat to find an ashtray or pick up a drink.

The last item of furniture that we are going to talk about today is side chairs. They are usually wooden, but they must be comfortable, movable, and sturdy. Be a chair ancient or modern, it must be strong. Fragile chairs are an enemy. They are an enemy of comfort and they are dangerous. Any time a large man breaks a delicate Chippendale chair, he should not have the slightest feeling of guilt or embarrassment. The blame can be laid at the feet of the hostess, who may indeed be about to break her own neck on the tears she has shed on her threadbare carpet. In fact, if she is a lady that is exactly what she should do. Shame on her for putting out a flimsy chair and expecting her guests to sit in it.

Now we are ready to approach the exciting and limitless topic of color. We will also consider that color is not entirely limitless in its use. Much of the application of color depends on exposure—the light that comes through the windows when the room is to be used . . . Is it a day room or a room that will be used only at night? Finally, the most important thing to consider in selecting colors is to be sure that they are colors that you yourself love. Do not make these decisions with any thought of what is in fashion or what the decorator likes.

Color is completely and totally affected by light and colors next to it. Always choose a color on the walls of the room where it will be used and be sure that fabrics that will be used are available for consideration. Even when you think you have decided on

*The sunroom in the apartment of Mr. and Mrs. Harding Lawrence, New York. The paintings over the sofa are by Al Held. The woven wicker sled chairs were designed by Ward Bennett. Photo by Horst.*

the perfect color, it absolutely must be seen in the actual room, with the fabrics, in daylight and at night with artificial light. When you make these decisions, forget about exact matches. Think about harmony. I think that an exact match can be too tight.

Try using a color on the walls that is in a print that you are using or maybe a blend of colors from a print. Consider using an outside color on the walls—by this I mean a color that does not occur in the fabrics in the room. This can give a subtle relaxation to the room. Don't get your colors too tightly tied together. This will make the room look muscle-bound and over-schemed.

The one thing I urge you to do, please free yourself from fashion. If the decorating magazines are promoting blue and you prefer green, use green. If you love red and the color of the moment is orange, forget it and stick to your red. Remember, you are not buying a dress. You are arranging a place to live. This place should grow and become more and more charming as you live in it. Some women are such victims of fashion that they will buy a dress of a hot new color that is unbecoming to them just because it is in style. At least the dress can be disposed of at the end of the season when it is out of style. Remember this: your favorite color is never out of style. It can become your trademark, you possess the color. The color does not possess you.

The impressionists freed us from the somber colors of the Victorians and the Edwardians. I feel that I owe all of my color sense to Henri Matisse. More than anyone, he taught me about fresh, clean color and the use of white. If you are cautious or afraid of color, don't forget the eighteenth century. The people in that cold, tough, civilized age were color mad. To see this just look at the underside of a piece of needlepoint from that period or turn over a carpet that was used in the eighteenth century. The original colors

that you will see are brilliant. We have come to believe that the faded colors displayed in museums and the houses of collectors is what these people liked. Not so! The original colors were so bright that today we would say they bordered on being gaudy. Look at the underside of embroidered silk garments worn in the eighteenth century. Again you will find the original bright, fresh colors that have not faded through the years. Having said all of this, I am not particularly interested in antiques or old things. Give me colors that are bright, newborn.

When you select colors, think about a few of the basics that hold true; for example, if you want a room painted in a brilliant lettuce green, you have set the color scale for the entire room. All of the furnishings, rugs, and curtains will be selected to go with, and be in harmony with, lettuce green. Another color truism to keep in mind is that dark colors, for example green or brown, are best in shiny gloss paint. Matte brown looks like a fallen chocolate soufflé. It is true that high-gloss paint on the walls brings out all of the cracks and imperfections, but lighting fixtures, mirrors, and pictures break them up so they can't be traced very far.

Pale colors and soft colors are better in flat paint. When I use these colors, I prefer them with white doors and woodwork that is painted an eggshell-enamel finish. Any time there is a chimneypiece, it must be white, natural pine, or even black. Never paint the chimneypiece the color of the walls. I am thankful that we have gotten away from classifying colors into "living room colors" and "bedroom colors." The same is true for wallpaper. As far as I am concerned, the only question to ask about a bedroom is, "Do the husband and wife like the color?" The one thing I would never choose for a bedroom is green bed linens, but that is a personal prejudice on my part.

I do think that colorless rooms lack a certain vitality. I mean rooms that are painted all white, pale gray,

and dull browns. These colors require a variety of textures—lots of books or pictures. Giving dimension to the walls helps personalize what would otherwise be a clinical, antiseptic atmosphere. Certainly there was never anything sterile about the wonderful white rooms created by Syrie Maugham in the thirties. That is because she knew how to use texture. Rooms were never more brilliant than when they were in her hands. Over the years, imitators have made a mess of what Syrie Maugham did, but then this is true of anyone who does imitations. The white rooms that people do today have no heart and soul in them.

At the opposite end of the spectrum is Rose Cumming, who was the greatest colorist in the history of American interior decorating. The magic she created was instinctive and passionate. The kind of genius Rose Cumming had cannot be taught. Try as people may, her gift for understanding the use of color can never successfully be inculcated. To even begin to understand color, you have to understand that color is one of the few things in life that is free. No one color costs more than another color, but I urge you, please, handle this priceless gift with love and care.

We now come to fabrics. We are spoiled by the overwhelming variety of fabrics on the market today. There is almost too much for us to choose from. I never take a client to a fabric house. The experience is confusing to the untrained eye. You should expect your decorator to be your editor and bring to you what is suitable for your job. It is the decorator's job to present to the client fabrics within the budget and to say how they will be used. This is what you are paying your decorator to do.

I do not like fabrics that look too expensive. My favorite fabric is cotton. It is fresh, vital, unpretentious, and practical. Cotton goes with everything—modern or antique, gilt or wicker. It comes in so many textures—glazed and unglazed chintz; shears; corduroy; both tightly and loosely woven. There is no end to the

range of colors that are available in cotton fabrics. Remember that Madame Pompadour, who had the most exquisite taste of her day and was responsible for introducing Louis XV furniture to France, had an entire apartment at Castle Bellevue decorated in white and indigo blue India cotton. Today, sturdy cotton denim is the very best blue on earth.

Now I want to talk about windows. My only complaint about modern architecture is the lack of beautiful windows. Many modern houses have entire walls of glass. In other words, the entire house is all windows. But I am talking about the beautiful-proportioned eighteenth century windows found in French, English, and colonial American architecture. Aside from the glory of the window frame itself, the beautiful detail of the moldings, I am talking about the way the window frames the view beyond.

I know that contemporary architecture with vast expanses of glass offers some spectacular views, but I think it is better when the view is controlled by a frame—the window frame. Views need frames in the same way that pictures do. Be assured that I accept and appreciate great contemporary abstract paintings that have no frame. I do not want you to think that I am positively archaic, but to me nothing is more

*A sketch to illustrate Baldwin's theory of a room being decorated in black and white. Private collection.*

poetic than a long open window looking out to a field or the sea and a filmy curtain flowing in a gentle breeze. The movement of the fabric gives life to the room. I think it is a pity to be in a modern house looking out to the sea, and all you can feel is the breeze of the air conditioner. Why not stay in the city in your charming air-conditioned apartment.

More often than not you will need more than a wisp of a curtain for privacy, light control, and, on occasion, the re-proportioning of a window with ugly dimensions. Whatever your needs, I feel the best solution will come from using as little curtain as possible. Most of the glare in a room comes from the top of the window. To relieve this it is best to use a Roman shade or horizontal blinds and avoid side curtains that draw to the center of the window. Curtains that pull in and out will kill the glare, but they plunge the room into darkness. For people who are instantly awakened by the first crack of dawn's early light, I suggest opaque blinds that are made to cover the window to the outside trim.

Another solution for keeping out the early-morning light is to have draw curtains that hang from under a valance, with a roller shade covered in the same fabric as the wallpaper. When the shade is up, it should be under the valance and not seen. The curtains should be lined and inner lined. I am thinking about your comfort and the comfort of your guests. All of these suggestions are for window coverings in rooms used for sleeping. These solutions also add greatly to the quietness of a room.

In any room, the most practical and charming solution for window covering is adjustable louvered shutters. When they are installed you will no doubt think they cost a fortune, and it is very expensive, but remember, they last forever. There must be two pairs of shutters at each window. One pair covers the top half of the window, and the other pair, the bottom half. In the bathroom, for instance, open the top half for shaving or doing makeup. Keep the bottom half closed for privacy. This arrangement will give a glorious light in the room.

In addition to controlling light, curtains can serve to correct unpleasant or bad window proportions when they are extended beyond the frame or raised above it. While I do not favor valances, they can add height to a room when they are installed above the window. When a window is extremely wide, a valance becomes a connection between the panels on each side when the curtains are fully open. When the curtains are pulled back, the valance becomes an anchor. This is especially true when the curtain fabric contrasts dramatically with the surrounding wall. If you are using a hard valance, be sure that the wood is padded to soften the overall effect. I no longer use any passementerie on draperies, valances, or upholstered furniture. I never use fringe even in a period room. In fact, I cannot even think of doing a period room!

There are two schools of thought about curtains: Some people like curtains that are very tailored, others like them to have a dressmaker look. Both opinions are correct, but it is up to the client and the decorator, who should come to a good understanding early on. When you are choosing a pattern fabric for curtains, be sure that you bunch it together to see how it will look in folds at the window. Many patterns that are great when they are hanging straight or stretched tight on upholstery look heavy and dense when they are gathered. Always keep in mind that, during the day, the light is behind the fabric, not on the surface as with lamplight in the evening. Whatever you choose, keep in mind that today nobody wants stuffy, heavy draperies. That word, by the way, means draped curtains. We will not even discuss draperies.

In Paris in the thirties, it was the fashion to take the old tapestry fabric off of upholstered furniture, carefully store it away, and re-cover the pieces in pale satin. I think this was indeed a step in the right direction. I confess it was somewhat extreme but then most purges are. In a way, the same kind of fanaticism is happening in curtains today. Plain curtains are everywhere. It is a castration of sorts. There is no pattern anywhere, nothing for the eye to feast on. To omit all pattern without adding something in its place, such as strong and obvious variations of texture, is to remove the seasoning from a meal.

If a room is filled with books, many objects, and many pictures, there is a reason to consider furniture and draperies without pattern and creating a monotone. This is easy with slipcovers in all white, or gray,

*A sketch to illustrate Baldwin's theory of using pink with black and white. Private collection.*

or beige. The inexperienced decorator, or would-be decorator, will tell you that too much pattern makes a room too busy. It is only too busy if you lose your nerve and don't go all the way. If you are going to use a lot of pattern then really do it. Don't be timid.

Vita Sackville-West, one of England's greatest gardeners, said that there must not be one inch of uncovered soil in the garden. When you are applying her philosophy to patterned rooms, I think that pattern-on-pattern works much better in small rooms. When successfully done, these small rooms take on an intimate quality. Small rooms should be crowded. Large rooms should have more space and appear emptier. Pattern-on-pattern rooms are cluttered rooms. There is nothing wrong with that—the more that goes into them, the better. Keep ever in mind that the clutter must be controlled and immaculate. To decorate this kind of room requires discipline and knowledge. Many decorators think that any pattern goes with any pattern. This is not so. Some of the do-it-yourself ladies think that all of this is very easy and, that horrible word, amusing. It is not.

The art of decorating with many patterns is impossible to teach. I believe it must be instinctive. The rule that always applies is that the patterns must, in some way, be related. This can be achieved through texture, color or, perhaps, period. To use pattern successfully you must train your eye, not your mind. Begin by looking at books on Asian art, architecture, decoration, fashion, and costume design. Look carefully at the intricate designs found in Japanese, Persian, and East Indian art. Look at the small pictures of Édouard Vuillard. He painted little pictures of little rooms that were filled with little pictures on the walls. Look carefully at the work of Henri Matisse. Even his large canvases are filled with intricate patterns. As you learn to see, you will come to understand why an elaborate necklace from India can only be worn on a patterned dress. When your room is assembled, complete, and you realize that one pattern stands out, remove it. Every pattern in the room must work with all of the other patterns.

Now on to the subject of light. Ruby Ross Wood always said, "Where there is no light, there is no beauty." Well put! How right she was. What good is it to have a room that is lovely in the daylight but becomes a cavern at night. This is true about every aspect of decorating. Take a picture or painting, one that I hope you love, for example. What good is the picture if it is improperly lighted at night and, during the day, it is impossible to see because it hangs between two windows that give glaring light?

To sit in a dimly lit room in the evening, where people's faces are barely distinguishable, is not romantic. It is spooky. You feel that the room does not exist. On the other hand, flooding a room with too much light washes out the color and flattens all the nuances of shapes and patterns. The result of this room is a splitting headache. The well-lit room is subtly lighted. The light in the room is evenly diffused. Remember, light is, first and last, for seeing.

The worst possible light for reading is the one that is most commonly used: a tall lamp with a translucent shade that allows the light to shine right into your eyes. A reading light should shine on the page that you are reading. In a dining room, chandeliers should be nothing more than decoration. Nothing is more hideous than one with large, bright bulbs. The lights shine in your eyes, on your head, and everyone at the table looks like they are a hundred years old. Always use small candle bulbs and consider an indirect light shining on the chandelier. At the table it is nice to see what you are eating, but a blazing light takes away your appetite.

How paintings should be lighted is an endless argument. Ideally, you should not be conscious of the light. The test is to turn off the light and see if the painting disappears. The proper lighting of a painting depends on the color of the walls and the other lighting in the room. Art gallery dealers and decorators have quarreled about this for years. There are no general rules. Every painting requires different lighting.

When you are lighting a staircase be sure that the light is directed to where you will step. So often the light is directed to the ceiling, which is extremely hazardous. I hope that art lamps with elaborate shades are gone forever from living rooms. Forget about having a teapot wired for a lamp base, or worse, a golf trophy. A lamp is for giving light, not some artistic medium. I hope to see as few as possible of these. The more lampshades that you see, the more dated the room seems, and remember, no fashion changes quicker than lampshades. For me, I want a simple, totally modern spot lamp.

We can sum up the elements of decoration into three classifications: something to sit on, something to put on, something to look upon. From the time I could listen and understand, my grandmother told me, "You must be useful as well as ornamental and as ornamental as you are useful." This creed applies to all of the elements of design that we have discussed.

# The Personal Touch

Today I want to begin by telling you a story about Cole Porter. After Cole's wife, Linda, died, he commissioned me to decorate his new apartment in the Waldorf Towers. As soon as we had signed the contract, he left for an extended trip to Europe. Upon his return, when he stepped through the door of apartment 33A, he turned and said, "Billy, is all of this mine?" Indeed it was.

Cole had inherited everything from the estate of his late wife, which included many beautiful French antiques that she had lovingly collected in Paris before the Second World War. He had lived with the furniture for years but was scarcely aware of it. Now everything belonged to him and he felt a new sense of responsibility. Looking around the apartment, Cole said, "In order for a person to really possess the things that belong to him, that person must know and understand them."

Soon after moving into the new apartment, Cole pasted two charts, side by side, on his shaving mirror: one of the kings of England and the other of the kings of France. Memorizing the names of the kings and the dates of their reigns was the start of his education. He learned quickly and grew to be very knowl-edgeable about his treasures. He was proud of them not as status symbols but for the very fine things they were and because they belonged to him. Nothing, and I mean nothing, is interesting unless it is personal.

In painting, a great artist is one who has something to say. To be able to communicate, through his painting, the things that he wants to express can take years of experimenting. It can take a very long time for the artist to be able to put forth his ideas in his own way. It is as if a fire burns within him and the things he wants to express come with deep passion. This same fire must burn in composers, authors, and sculptors. We may look on this as a creative flowering. Nowhere is this more important than in the decorating of a room. I want us to think together about how this happens to create very personal rooms for a client.

First of all, I believe in mixing things up. By this I mean mixing the old and the new, mixing things that came from different places, even different countries. I know that a piece of antique furniture brings a quality to a room that nothing else does. Keep ever in mind that not all antiques are beautiful just because they are antiques.

The residence of Mr. and Mrs. John
King Reckford in Jamaica. The rooms
were designed by Ruby Ross Wood and
Baldwin in 1938. The trompe-l'œil
commode is one of a pair painted by
Joseph B. Platt. Photograph by Peter Nyholm.

I also know that some modern furniture, carefully selected, can be very good, and in time it will have the same effect as a fine antique. I am thinking about some of the modern designs that came out of the atelier of Jean-Michel Frank in the thirties. It takes a trained eye to discriminate between what is good and what is bad in these things that are being designed today. Nothing is more foolish than acquiring something, anything, just because it is different, a novelty. Very likely the novelty of today will be the bad taste of tomorrow. It is sad to see people invest a lot of money in a conversation piece (I think this is an unfortunate phrase) that provides something to talk about but quickly becomes unmentionable. Certainly it is by the end of the year—and should be. Let us hope that some of this personal enthusiasm can be controlled by an experienced decorator. And further, we hope that the decorator will put aside personal prejudice and logically and intelligently advise the client.

I want to repeat and stress that I like to mix things up. What I mean is that I like a mixture of what the client likes. I feel strongly that the introduction of something modern can work wonders in what I call "an established room." I believe that an old, broken-down butler's-tray coffee table should be thrown into the ash can and replaced by a simple contemporary one. I would even suggest something that is inspired by Chinese design. If the client has a lovely old butler's-tray table and, regardless of the condition, cannot give it up, I will say, "Use it." The client lives in the house, not me, and besides, nothing is worth having a family row.

Most people's taste today does run toward a mixture of furnishings. Gone are the period room and the ghastly museum look. Not so very long ago there was an epidemic among the very rich for fine French furniture. I call this FFF. When collecting FFF is carried to the extreme, it is the embodiment of snobbism, and the rooms where it is displayed look like a museum. When you are in such an atmosphere you feel that there should be a velvet rope across each door. You can almost feel the frost of these starkly cold rooms. These spaces do not beckon us to come in; they do not lure us into any enjoyment. More than

FACING PAGE AND BELOW

*Residence of Mr. and Mrs. John King Reckford, Jamaica. The rooms were designed by Ruby Ross Wood and Baldwin in 1938. All photographs by Peter Nyholm.*

just being French, there is a distance, an emotional foreignness, that repels us.

These frozen rooms are not of our age and we realize that they only speak of vast sums of money. Any normally intelligent person who has read and studied period furniture, and visited museums and antiques dealers—shall we say, a good student with wherewithal, unlimited cash funds—can put together these vulgar rooms. While some people may look at them and deem them perfect, I say they hold nothing personal—the most important thing in decorating—and their perfection has killed everything. There is one such "perfect" apartment in New York City [that] someone has brilliantly described as "a series of foyers leading to nothing." How sad to see rooms that could have been so beautiful but instead they are cold perfection. When you walk into the drawing room, and that is all you do, you realize there is no place to sit. Even the owner's master bedroom has the feeling of an unwelcoming guest room. I end this by saying this happens with other period furniture. It doesn't have to be eighteenth-century French. Try being comfortable in the rooms of someone who is a nut about colonial American furniture.

In the book *The Finest Rooms*, Mrs. Archibald Brown, the president of the great decorating firm, McMillen, Inc., wrote: "A contemporary house that ignores all vestiges of the past in order to express a purely modern philosophy runs the risk of becoming a stagnant document of its own time, lacking in vitality and becoming just as boring and unnatural as any "antique" period brought intact for today's living." I say, "Bravo, Mrs. Brown."

I think that perfection causes sterility. I much prefer a piece of furniture, a picture, or an object that is a part of the client's life—something that was bought when the purchase price was a real sacrifice but it was worth it and every year it becomes more so. I am not talking about intrinsic value, I am talking about joy. A chair may not be the most perfect from a decorative point of view but for the client it is the most loved. Just one week before the horrific tragedy in Dallas, Mrs. John F. Kennedy called me to help with the little house that she and the president had in Virginia. Later she said that I was polite not to mention the rocking chair in the living room. I responded that it was not a question of manners. I could not think of anything more presumptuous or less professional than a decorator suggesting that the favorite chair of the president of the United States should be removed from his living room.

A room that is perfect has no room to grow. I don't think a room should ever be finished. I feel the same way about gardens. There are some people who, a week after they move in, make their house look like they've lived there for years. Other people live in their house for years and it looks like they just moved in. Whenever I finish a job, I know that there are some things that only the client and time can accomplish. I've done several houses for one client, and every time I visit one of them she says, "Aren't you proud? We haven't touched one thing. It is all just like you left it."

Another client is just the opposite. When the furniture is in place, the curtains hung, the pictures and wall fixtures hung, and the books are in place, this lady and I smile at each other in mutual admiration. I then say to her, "All right, you know what it needs, go ahead and mess it up." She will then add her personal objects, perhaps hang another picture or two, create a new needlepoint pillow, arrange some flowers from her garden, and even move a chair or two to places that are more convenient. She feels free to break up the hardness of the decorator's perfect look. She knows how to make the room her own and give it her personal stamp.

A great friend of this woman imitates everything that she does. The poor thing doesn't have bad taste, she simply has no taste at all. To make matters worse, she is not one bit domestic. I can only smile when I go into her bedroom. The dear woman has a big heart—she sees everything and has a terrific memory. On an enchanting Regency sewing table there is a bag of needlepoint that has been there, in exactly the same place, for three years. She keeps it there because her friend does needlepoint, but this woman hasn't the patience to even begin a piece of needlepoint. On the same table, just like her friend, she has a small picture of the needlepoint artist. She is a nice woman but [in] her house, all of the rooms add up to nothing. The whole thing is a fake, a copy. If indeed imitation is the most sincere form of flattery, then her friend should feel very complimented.

Any collection of anything must be made by the collector himself. Collections come with study, hard work, and learning. Without these, a collection has no meaning; it is mere decoration. It can be embarrassing to inquire about the origins of a coin collection in a cabinet and have the host say, "I really don't know anything about it, my decorator bought those."

What we remember about rooms is the atmosphere, the mood. Unless rooms are personal, they have none of this. Rooms must be economically suitable for the occupant and provide a space that can be suitably used. The only trace a decorator should leave in a room is the knowledge that he imparts to the client through the long experience of their working together. There should be no indication that the decorator's taste has been imposed on the room. If you want clutter, you should have clutter and hire a decorator who arranges it so that you love it even more. If you want space, lots and lots of space, do not let the decorator get in your way.

When I think back on the rooms of my childhood and dream about the past, it is memories of objects that are the most nostalgic. In my early years, we called them ornaments and they were kept in the front parlor. The doors of the room were always closed. The parlor was a place of mystery. I wasn't supposed to ever go into the room alone, but I did, and I would just stand and look at the precious objects, the ornaments on the tabletops. I remember one was a bust of a beautiful woman in snow white bisque. Another was a silver violin imported from Germany.

On one table was a multicolored cache pot decorated with life-size plums in full relief. On one wall was a china cabinet filled with things too fragile for the parlor maid to handle. My mother dusted these things herself. I was thrilled to watch her. Each time it was like the first time, as though I had never seen these things before. All of the things were selected by my mother and father, or were gifts to each other on birthdays and anniversaries. These objects were their collection. Every piece was personal, something that they loved. Today I have no idea what happened to these things.

The pictures on your walls should be the most personal things you own. Sadly, this is not always true.

*The living room in the apartment of*
*Mr. and Mrs. Lee Eastman in New*
*York City. Painting on the left by*
*Willem de Kooning, and on the right*
*by Franz Kline.* Photo by Horst.

LEFT AND FACING PAGE
*Residence of Mrs. John Wintersteen in Pennsylvania. The painting above the sofa in this picture is by Picasso.* Photo by Horst.

Many pictures are hung because they are status symbols, things done by famous people, and have been acquired solely for their value as investments. I think it is shameful to be taken around a room and have a host whisper in my ear how much was paid for this or that picture. Sometimes it is bellowed for all in the room to hear!

Pictures should be loved and only people who do love their pictures should be allowed to have them. When someone truly loves their art collection, you know it because it is an emotion that cannot be faked. I have often enjoyed the thrilling experience of going to art galleries with my clients. I have never encour-

aged them to select a picture because it fits a decorating scheme or because the colors are right. When this happens, you run the risk of the picture disappearing in the room or being suffocated by the colors around it. A picture is primarily a work of art, not a decoration. When a room has been assembled and you need a picture, consider first and foremost what the room does for the picture—not what the picture does for the room. Finally, I have never bought a picture for a client that she has not seen and is not pleased with.

I find it very refreshing to go into a room and see a picture that is completely new to me. It is like meet-

FACING PAGE AND ABOVE

*Studio apartment of the writer Speed Lamkin in New York City. They illustrate one of Baldwin's favorite decorating schemes: walls of shirred curtains.* Photo by Horst.

FACING PAGE

*The entrance hall in the residence of Mr. and Mrs. James Fentress, in Florida. Photo by Norman Parkinson.*

ing an intriguing total stranger. I see it, digest it, and I quite naturally ask, "Who is this painter? Tell me about him or her. Where can I see more of his work?" The whole experience is like someone giving me a gift. I feel the same way about small pictures that are displayed on tabletops. They provide the pleasure of a treasure hunt. If you are in a room waiting for your hostess to arrive, looking at her pictures is the most rewarding snooping you can do. Seeing how extremely personal art is, you should realize that you never, ever give someone a picture unless you know they are longing to have it. If you see a picture you really love, buy it. You will find a place for it—maybe not the place you had in mind when you bought it. And it may even end up in another room. I find that my pictures are the things I move around the most and they never seem to be upset at all.

Moving day is always a good time to reassess what your pictures mean to you. How much do you really like them? Ask yourself some questions about them: Have you outgrown some of them or are they not nearly so appealing as they once were? [Don't make your sweep to clean.] Pictures that people have loved and cared for are a bigger part of their life than they often realize. More than anything else, your pictures will make you feel at home in your new house or apartment. This does not mean that you will hang or group them as you did before. They may even be in a different room. If you are moving into a smaller place, your pictures may look friendlier and more relaxed in their reduced circumstances.

Briefly, I want us to think about photographs. I personally like to see them on tables in any room, but I prefer to see a lot of them grouped on a tabletop in small rooms. I think they work better in a confined space as opposed to a large room. Having said this, in just a minute I will tell you about a very large room where photographs worked well. Here I want to say that I like to see photographs used in a group on the walls of a library. They become the family album. The only picture that I think should be removed from the drawing room of any house and put in a more private place is the very large picture of a smiling bride, usually the lady of the house, taken far too many years ago. Invariably it is sitting on the piano. This picture goes!

Now to the big room with photographs. Some years ago I worked with a bachelor at his enormous house on Long Island. He had a tremendous living room filled with museum-quality eighteenth-century English furniture. On the walls were great paintings of the same period. Elegantly displayed in the room were very fine pieces of porcelain, and the uphol-stered furniture was covered almost entirely in blue-and-white chintz. In order to get to the library of the house, where he usually entertained, it was necessary to walk through this absolutely beautiful drawing room. As striking as the room was, there was no temptation to pause or linger. The room was very cold, which was a tragedy. One day I suggested that we might put a few photographs on some of the absolutely superb tables. When I went to the house about a month later, the mission was accomplished. In matching large shining gold frames, thoughtfully placed around the room, there were life-size heads of some of his closest friends: the duke and duchess of Windsor, President Eisenhower, Cardinal Spellman, and Ethel Merman. It was a great success, and yes, from then on people very much wanted to have a look around the room.

I have always contended that books are the best decoration of all. Certainly there is not a room in the house where they do not fit. I will confess that I can-

not see them in a room that is used only for eating. It is very difficult to eat and read. Having said this, I also feel that people who do not read should not fill their apartments with books just to appear intellectual. These people should fill their apartments with evidence of the things that do interest them. I have even known people who go to book dealers and buy their books by the yard; they have no intention of ever reading them. These books, usually in handsome leather bindings, add a warmth and glow to a room, but for all of the atmosphere they exude, I say, "Why not buy wooden panels that are covered with fake book spines in real hand-tooled leather? Wouldn't it be the same thing?"

When you are planning your house or apartment, you cannot have too many bookshelves. I love to see doors and windows that are completely surrounded with books—on the sides and over the top. It looks like a door has been cut right through the wall of books. It is nice to find that every time you visit people they have added a few more bookcases since you were last there. These new bookcases spring up in guest rooms, guest bathrooms, and are often tucked away on a second floor hallway.

Having told you how much I like bookcases, I want to add that I hate breakfronts. I also don't like to see books arranged on shelves that also display porcelain birds and plates on stands. I think the books lose their integrity and become secondary decorative objects. I have, on occasion, seen bronze busts and small bronze figures interspersed among books. The color of the metal is harmonious with books, but remember, if you do this, do not use the figures for bookends.

I do not think that bookcases should have glass doors or doors with metal grills unless the volumes are extremely rare and perishable. If they are, then the books should also be under lock and key. I feel very strongly that they should be clearly visible and anyone should feel free to take a book and enjoy it in one's room. Here, I remind the reader, if you take a book to your room, always return it to the shelf where you got it.

Books on coffee tables are great but not "coffee table" books. These large, oversize books just sit there year after year. I like to see books on the coffee table that are about all subjects: politics, ecology, the latest book of fiction, the book of the moment. These books give the house energy; they become conversation pieces.

In the very first lecture, I talked about the importance of harmony between the husband, the wife, the architect, and the decorator. We are in the last lecture and I still feel very strongly about this. Now I want to tell you about the greatest menace in decorating: the friend with taste. Often this menace is a decorator, or at least she thinks she is. If she isn't, she will usually tell you that all of her friends think she should have been a decorator. Smugly, she thinks that the world is missing quite a lot because she has resisted her vocation. She seldom comes to the first meeting you have with your client. She wants to be sitting next to the client for the fun part: the colors, the fabrics, the wallpapers.

This menace is far more definite than the client. She talks loudly and prances around the room draping samples of fabric over chairs. She constantly says to the client, "I don't want to say anything, but you did ask me to be here and to feel free to express my opinions."

247

And she does. One of these women once said to me, "I just love what you did for Sally Smith, except for that rug. Really, Mr. Baldwin." Another of these miserable offenders said, "I know that you did your best with Betty, but it was naughty of you to have allowed her to buy that ghastly chintz." Finally, there was the one who said, "Well of course, the Joneses have ruined that beautiful room you did for them by hanging that horrible Rothko. I just hate abstract art." Do not listen to these people. You want your rooms to be yours and have your taste and personality. They should not reflect the ideas of your friends. When these opinionated creatures have shown up on a job that I am doing, I assure you they are not there for long. I simply say to the client that she must never, ever bring that woman within my range of vision again. Whenever I am working with a husband and wife together, I have never had one of these know-it-all women appear.

Once many years ago when I was working with Mrs. Wood, a client carrying an enormous roll of blue-prints came in for an appointment. With a charming smile she said, "Oh, Mrs. Wood, I do hope that when we have finished, my whole house will look like Dorothy Draper did it." Mrs. Wood, not smiling, said to me, "Mr. Baldwin, will you please give this lady the address of Mrs. Draper's office and show her to the elevator."

The sad truth of this story is that many people buy something not because they love it but because they think people will notice their new purchase. They want recognition, and they hope people will talk about how daring they were to buy this new thing. In the end, this works against a person. You should never be so aware of a room that it comes between you and the other people in the room. Rather than appropriate interior decoration, what you see is interference.

I would always want to see less and less studied decoration and more and more things that have been chosen because you love them. You being at home with the things you like best is the whole point. Having the colors that make you happy, fabrics that you like, and furniture that you find the most comfortable—in a word, things that matter to you—is what successful interior decorating is all about.

Each spring and fall, the editors of magazines would call me and say, "What colors are you using?" Even worse, they would ask, "What colors are they using?" I always wondered who "they" were. If I did know these people that are "they," how could I know what they were using until I saw their work—rooms that were finished.

These same editors would also ask, "What are the trends?" *Trends* is a word I hate. The inventions of manufacturers, trends are used to promote business. Trends are the death knell of the personal stamp in decorating. If I found that something that I was doing had become a trend, I would run from it like the plague. If you are a decorator and have a client who is a slave to fashion and won't spend any money, get rid of her. If you have a decorator that is a slave to fashion and thinks only of making money, get rid of him.

In the end, decorating is all about color. Think about colored flowers on bright white cotton and, in the same room, right next to this celebration of color, is more color—fresh flowers, lots of them. To each of you I send a huge bouquet of brightly colored cotton flowers. Thank you.

# Bibliography

Amory, Cleveland and Frederic Bradlee, eds. *Vanity Fair: A Cavalcade of the 1920s and 1930s*. New York: Viking, 1960.

Astor, Brooke. *Footprints, An Autobiography*. Garden City, New York: Doubleday & Company, Inc., 1980.

Auchincloss, Louis. *Edith Wharton: A Woman in Her Time*. New York: Viking, 1971.

Aylesworth, Thomas G. and Virginia. *New York: The Glamour Years (1919–1945)*. New York: Gallery Books, 1987.

Baldwin, William W. *Billy Baldwin Decorates*. New York: Holt, Rinehart, and Winston, 1973.

Baldwin, William W. *Billy Baldwin Remembers*. New York: Harcourt Brace Jovanovich, 1974.

Ballard, Bettina. *In My Fashion*. New York: David McKay Company, Inc., 1960.

Bartlett, Apple Parish, and Susan Bartlett Crater. *Sister*. New York: St. Martin's Press, 2000.

Battersby, Martin, revised by Philippe Garner. *The Decorative Thirties*. New York: Whitney Library of Design, 1988.

Battersby, Martin, revised by Philippe Garner. *The Decorative Twenties*. New York: Whitney Library of Design, 1988.

Beaton, Cecil. *The Best of Beaton*. New York: Macmillan, 1968.

Beaton, Cecil. *Cecil Beaton's Scrapbook*. New York: Scribner's, 1937.

Beaton, Cecil. *Memoirs of the '40s*. London: Weidenfeld and Nicolson, 1972.

Beaton, Cecil, and Kenneth Tynan. *Persona Grata*. New York: G.P. Putnam's, 1954.

Beaton, Cecil. *The Glass of Fashion*. Garden City, New York: Doubleday, 1954.

Becker, Robert. *Nancy Lancaster: Her Life, Her World, Her Art*. New York: Alfred A. Knopf, 1996.

Bernier, Georges and Rosamund, eds. *European Decoration: Creative Contemporary Interiors*. New York: William Morrow, 1969.

Brown, Erica. *Sixty Years of Interior Design: The World of McMillen*. New York: Viking, 1982.

Brunhammer, Yvonne and Suzanne Tise. *The Decorative Arts in France, 1900–1942*. New York: Rizzoli, 1990.

Cameron, Roderick. *The Golden Riviera*. London: Weidenfeld and Nicolson, 1975.

Chauncey, George. *Gay New York: Gender, Urban Culture, and the Making of the Gay Male World, 1890–1940*. New York: Basic Books, 1994.

Comstock, Helen. *100 Most Beautiful Rooms in America*. New York: Bonanza Books, 1958.

Core, Philip. *The Original Eye: Arbiters of Twentieth-Century Taste*. London: Quartet Books, 1984.

Cowles, Fleur, ed. *The Best of Flair*. New York: HarperCollins, 1996.

Curtis, Charlotte. *The Rich and Other Atrocities*. New York: Harper & Row, 1976.

de Wolfe, Elsie. *After All*. New York: Harper & Brothers, 1935.

de Wolfe, Elsie. *The House in Good Taste*. New York: Century, 1914.

Donovan, Carrie. *Living Well: the New York Times Book of Home Design and Decoration*. New York: Times Books, 1981.

Fisher, Richard B. *Syrie Maugham*. London: Duckworth, 1978.

Foucart, Bruno, and Jean-Louis Gaillemin. *Les Décorateurs des années 40*. Paris: Norma Editions, 1998.

Gardine, Michael. *Billy Baldwin: An Autobiography*. Boston: Little, Brown, 1985.

Gray, Susan. *Designers on Designers*. New York: McGraw-Hill, 2003.

Hadley, Albert, Sister Parish and Christopher Petkanas. *Parish-Hadley*. New York: Little, Brown, 1995.

Hall, Carolyn. *The Forties in Vogue*. New York: Harmony, 1985.

Hall, Carolyn. *The Thirties in Vogue*. New York: Harmony, 1985.

Hall, Carolyn. *The Twenties in Vogue*. New York: Harmony, 1983.

Hampton, Mark. *Legendary Decorators of the Twentieth Century*. New York: Doubleday, 1992.

Holme, Bryan, et al., ed. *The World in Vogue*. New York: Viking Press, 1963.

Jones, Chester. *Colefax and Fowler: The Best in English Interior Decoration*. New York: Little, Brown, and Company, 1989.

Kaiser, Charles. *The Gay Metropolis: 1940–1996*. New York: Houghton Mifflin, 1997.

Lawford, Valentine. *Horst, His Work and His World*. New York: Knopf, Inc., 1984.

Lawford, Valentine. *Vogue's Book of Houses, Gardens, People*. New York: Viking, 1968.

Leddick, David. *Intimate Companions: A Triography of George Platt Lynes, Paul Cadmus, Lincoln Kirstein, and Their Circle*. New York: St. Martin's Press, 2000.

Lewis, Adam. *Albert Hadley: The Story of America's Preeminent Interior Designer*. New York: Rizzoli International Publications, 2005.

Lewis, Adam. *The Great Lady Decorators*. New York: Rizzoli International Publications, 2010.

Lewis, Adam. *Van Day Truex: The Man Who Defined Twentieth-Century Taste and Style*. New York: Viking Press, 2001.

Mann, Carol. *Paris Between the Wars*. New York: Vendome, 1996.

Mann, William J. *Wisecracker: The Life and Times of William Haines, Hollywood's First Openly Gay Star*. New York: Viking, 1998.

Marquis, Alice Goldfarb. *Alfred H. Barr, Jr.: Missionary of the Modern*. Chicago: Contemporary Books, 1989.

Metcalf, Pauline. *C. Ogden Codman and the Decoration of Houses*. Boston: Boston Athenæum and Godine, 1988.

Morris, Janet. *Manhattan '45*. New York: Oxford University Press, 1987.

Pahlmann, William. *The Pahlmann Book of Interior Design*. New York: Crowell, 1955.

Parsons, Frank Alvah. *Interior Decoration, Its Principles and Practice*. New York: Doubleday, 1915.

Pohorilenko, Anatole, and James Crump. *When We Were Three: The Travel Albums of George Platt Lynes, Monroe Wheeler, and Glenway Wescott, 1925–1935*. Santa Fe, New Mexico: Arena Editions, 1998.

Pool, Mary Jane, ed. *20th Century Decorating, Architecture & Gardens: 80 Years of Ideas and Pleasure from* House and Garden. New York: Holt, Rinehart and Winston, 1980.

Praz, Mario. *The House of Life*. New York: Oxford University Press, 1964.

Robsjohn-Gibbings, T. H. *Good-bye, Mr. Chippendale*. New York: Knopf, 1944.

Robsjohn-Gibbings, T. H. *Homes of the Brave*. New York: Knopf, 1954

Ross, Josephine. *Society in Vogue*. New York: Vendome, 1992.

Ross Goodnow, Ruby, with Rayne Adams. *The Honest House*. New York: The Century Co., 1914.

de Rothschild, Pauline. *The Irrational Journey*. New York: Harcourt, Brace & World, 1966.

Rowlands, Penelope. *A Dash of Daring: Carmel Snow and Her Life in Fashion, Art, and Letters*. New York: Atria Books, 2005.

Salny, Stephen. *Frances Elkins*. New York: W. W. Norton & Company, 2005.

Snow, Carmel, with Mary Louise Aswell. *The World of Carmel Snow*. New York: McGraw-Hill, 1962.

Tapert, Annette, and Diana Edkins. *The Power of Style*. New York: Crown, 1994.

Tate, Allen, and C. Ray Smith. *Interior Design in the 20th Century*. New York: Harper & Row, 1986.

Tauranac, John, and Christopher Little. *Elegant New York: The Builders and the Buildings*. New York: Abbeville, 1985.

Trocmé, Suzanne. *Influential Interiors: Shaping 20th-Century Style Through Key Interior Designers*. New York: Clarkson-Potter, 1999.

Truex, Van Day. *Interiors, Character and Color*. Los Angeles: Knapp, 1980.

Tweed, Katharine, ed. *The Finest Rooms by America's Great Decorators*. New York: Viking Press, 1964.

Vreeland, Diana. *Allure*. Garden City, New York: Doubleday, 1980.

Vreeland, Diana. *D.V.* New York: Knopf, 1984.

Weeks, Christopher. *"Perfectly Delightful": The Life and Gardens of Harvey Ladew*. Baltimore: Johns Hopkins University Press, 1999.

Wharton, Edith, and Ogden Codman, Jr. *The Decoration of Houses*. New York: Norton, 1978.

Wood, Martin. *John Fowler: Prince of Decorators*. London: Frances Lincoln, 2007.

# Index

## ABOUT THE AUTHOR

Adam Lewis is an interior decorator and the author of *Van Day Truex: The Man Who Defined Twentieth-Century Taste and Style*, *Albert Hadley: America's Preeminent Interior Designer*, and *The Great Lady Decortors: The Women Who Defined Interior Design, 1870–1955*. Lewis is a graduate of the Yale School of Art and Architecture. He also studied at Parsons School of Design. He lives in New York City and Bridgehampton, Long Island.

First published in the United States of America in 2010
by Rizzoli International Publications, Inc.
300 Park Avenue South
New York, NY 10010
www.rizzoliusa.com

2010 2011 2012 2013 / 10 9 8 7 6 5 4 3 2 1

Distributed in the U.S. trade by Random House, New York

Designed by Abigail Sturges
Printed in China

ISBN-13: 978-0-8478-3367-2

Library of Congress Catalog Control Number: 2010927316

## PHOTOGRAPHY CREDITS

Condé Nast Archive; Copyright © Condé Nast Publications
Pages 1, 2, 5, 6,.9, 13, 17, 18, 21, 24, 68, 73, 74, 80, 81, 84, 86, 88, 89, 91, 97, 98, 100,101, 102, 103, 104, 105, 108, 111, 112, 113, 114, 116, 117, 125, 128,130, 137, 138,150, 152,153, 170, 178, 178, 207, 208, 209, 210, 212, 213, 214, 216, 217, 218, 219, 220, 221, 223, 225, 231, 232, 233, 234, 236, 238, 240, 241, 242, 243.

Evergreen Museum & Library, The John Hopkins University
Pages 32, 34, 35

Hearst Corporation, House Beautiful
Pages 26, 155, 156, 157, 158, 167

Ladew Topiary Gardens, Monkton, Maryland
Page 64

Museum of the City of New York
Gottscho-Schleisner Collection
Pages 180, 182, 183, 184, 185 187

The Lectures, "Decorating Today"
Smithsonian Institution Archives
Record Unit 267, Box Number #39

*Above: Painting by Jean Pagés.*